D0442938

For:

_____

From the fullness of his grace
we have all received
one blessing after another.

John 1:16

From:

_____

Requests for information should be addressed to:

✠ZondervanPublishingHouse
  Grand Rapids, Michigan 49530
  http://www.zondervan.com

Senior Editor: Gwen Ellis
Project Editor: Pat Matuszak
Designer: John Lucas
Composition: Big Cat

Printed in China
99 00 01 /HK / 4   3

Grace
for a
Woman's Soul

Reflections to
Renew Your Spirit

Zondervan*Gifts*

We have a gift for inspiration™

$\mathcal{W}$herever there are women of faith, you will find diversity. Today's Christian women live in all kinds of cities and towns, enjoy widely varying ethnic and family backgrounds, and career choices. They go to a host of different churches. They attend all kinds of Bible study groups and go to lots of conferences. Yet they all agree about one thing—God's grace has brought them from where they were yesterday to where they are today, and it will lead them into the future.

God's grace is a free gift that we can receive with gratitude. We can open it and clothe ourselves with it. His grace is big enough to cover all our failings. It's wide enough to make room for all who want to come into his family. It's deep enough to hold onto in the dark times of life. It's long enough to take us to eternity. And it's here, right now, in the present. It's for today! As you open this book, open your heart to what God has in store for you right now.

Table of Contents

Chapter One-*Grace*

Chapter Two-*Grace Gives Us...*

Chapter Three-*God's Grace in Our Lives Transforms Us*

Chapter Four-*God's Grace Extended Through Us*

Grace

Grace Is Available to All

❧

God's grace is a free gift that is available to everyone. It cannot be earned, learned, or churned up on our own. All we can do is receive it as we would a wonderful present from our very best friend. When we learn that God himself is holding out a gift so special that his Son gave his life to make sure of its delivery, what else can we do but humbly receive the amazing wonder that he went to such great lengths to purchase on our behalf?

There is an ache within my soul,
A longing deep as rivers roll,
An ancient song, a song of praise,
To hear your voice and see your face. . .
And I shall walk upon this earth
Until my journey finds its end;
Then I shall stand by amazing grace,
And hear your voice and see your face.

 Sheila Walsh

For if the many died by the trespass of the one man, how much more did God's grace and the gift that came by the grace of the one man, Jesus Christ, overflow to the many!

       ℜ Romans 5:15

Every good and perfect gift is from above, coming down from the Father of the heavenly lights, who does not change like shifting shadows. He chose to give us birth through the word of truth, that we might be a kind of firstfruits of all he created.

       ℜ James 1:17

God's gift to us of grace through his Son, Jesus was the first gift of Christmas.
When they saw the star, they were overjoyed. On coming to the house, they saw the child with his mother Mary, and they bowed down and worshiped him. Then they opened their treasures and presented him with gifts of gold and of incense and of myrrh.

       ℜ Matthew 2:10–11

Thanks be to God for his indescribable gift!

       ℜ 2 Corinthians 9:15

*W*hen we went on our first women's renewal weekend, my friends and I from our little prayer circle group weren't used to seeing so many women from other denominations all singing and praying together. They were so expressive and didn't question each other's background or ask what church they came from. It was just joy overflowing. I guess we really came with open hearts and made a decision to let go and let God do whatever work needed to be done in our lives.

Woman of Faith participant,
Sarah Evans

Rejoice in the Lord always. I will say it again: Rejoice! Let your gentleness be evident to all. The Lord is near.

Philippians 4:4–5

I will be glad and rejoice in you; I will sing praise to your name, O Most High

Psalm 9:2

*B*y night when others soundly slept
And hath at once both ease and Rest,
My waking eyes were open kept
And so to lie I found it best.

I sought him whom my Soul did Love,
With tears I sought him earnestly.
He bow'd his ear down from Above.
In vain I did not seek or cry.

My hungry Soul he fill'd with Good;
He in his Bottle put my tears,
My smarting wounds washt in his blood,
And banisht thence my Doubts and fears.

What to my Saviour shall I give
Who freely hath done this for me?
I'll serve him here whilst I shall live
And Love him to Eternity.

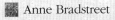 Anne Bradstreet

*W*hen we have hope, we can look at the big picture—God's promise of eternal life—rather than focus on our mistakes. When seen from that perspective it's easy to see that no matter what happens to us—or what havoc we unintentionally wreak on others—we will be able to learn from our mistakes and start over. We'll even be able to do what we never thought we could do: laugh again.

Barbara Johnson

For God so loved the world that he gave his one and only Son, that whoever believes in him shall not perish but have eternal life.

John 3:16

Now there was a man of the Pharisees named Nicodemus, a member of the Jewish ruling council.
He came to Jesus at night and said, "Rabbi, we know you are a teacher who has come from God. For no one could perform the miraculous signs you are doing if God were not with him."
In reply Jesus declared, "I tell you the truth, no one can see the kingdom of God unless he is born again."
"How can a man be born when he is old?" Nicodemus asked. "Surely he cannot enter a second time into his mother's womb to be born!"
Jesus answered, "I tell you the truth, no one can enter the kingdom of God unless he is born of water and the Spirit. Flesh gives birth to flesh, but the Spirit gives birth to spirit.
You should not be surprised at my saying, 'You must be born again.'

❧John 3:1–7

*J*ust as I am, without one plea
But that Thy blood was shed for me,
And that Thou bidd'st me come to Thee,
O Lamb of God, I come! I come!

Just as I am, and waiting not
To rid my soul of one dark blot,
To Thee whose blood can cleanse
each spot,
O Lamb of God, I come! I come!

Just as I am tho' tossed about
With many a conflict, many a doubt,
Fightings within and fears without
O Lamb of God, I come! I come!

*J*ust as I am, poor wretched blind;
Sight, riches, healing of the mind,
Yea, all I need in Thee to find,
O Lamb of God, I come! I come!

Just as I am, Though wilt receive
Wilt welcome, pardon, cleanse, relieve,
Because Thy promise I believe,
O Lamb of God, I come! I come!

Just as I am, Thy love unknown
Hath broken ev'ry barrier down;
Now to be Thine, yea, Thine alone,
O Lamb of God, I come! I come!

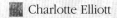 Charlotte Elliott

*B*e attentive, keep your eye on the sky, your feet on the ground and your heart tilted heavenward. When joy is deep within us, we will walk through this life with a lifted heart, soul, and mind. One day, one outrageous day, we will see on the horizon the Son rise. This, friends, will be more stunning, more thrilling, more exhilarating than a New Mexico sky teeming with hot air balloons. Until then, enjoy the view. It's the greatest show on earth.

Patsy Clairmont

God has shown kindness by giving you rain from heaven and crops in their seasons; he provides you with plenty of food and fills your hearts with joy.

Acts 14:17

For God did not send his Son into the world to condemn the world, but to save the world through him.

❧John 3:17

You see, at just the right time, when we were still powerless, Christ died for the ungodly.
Very rarely will anyone die for a righteous man, though for a good man someone might possibly dare to die.
But God demonstrates his own love for us in this: While we were still sinners, Christ died for us.
Since we have now been justified by his blood, how much more shall we be saved from God's wrath through him!
For if, when we were God's enemies, we were reconciled to him through the death of his Son, how much more, having been reconciled, shall we be saved through his life!
Not only is this so, but we also rejoice in God through our Lord Jesus Christ, through whom we have now received reconciliation.

❧Romans 5:6–11

Grace

$\mathcal{G}$race was never meant to be rationed—something we nibble on to get us through tough times. It is meant to soak us to, and through the skin and fill us so full that we can hardly catch our breath.

Then came a glorious morning when my pastor said, "There are some of you here today who feel like dead people staring up at the top of your own locked coffin. This morning, Jesus wants to set you free. You simply have to let go of the key and pass it through the little hole, where you see a tiny shaft of light."

I walked to the altar, dragging my shame and grief behind me. I knelt, with my head in my hands and lead weights on my feet, and, at the foot of the cross, confessed my utter hopelessness and helplessness to Christ and asked him to forgive me. It was as if Jesus himself were standing before me with outstretched arms, saying, "Welcome home, child, welcome home."

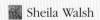 Sheila Walsh

We know and rely on the love God has for us. God is love. . . . We love because he first loved us.

✢1 John 4:16,19

"As the heavens are higher than the earth, so are my ways higher than your ways and my thoughts than your thoughts. . . . so is my word that goes out from my mouth:
It will not return to me empty, but will accomplish what I desire and achieve the purpose for which I sent it," declares the LORD.

✢Isaiah 55:9–11

*H*is grace is not only available to all—he uses anyone and everyone with a willing heart to bring it into someone's else's life special delivery!

God used common folks for the most sacred, esteemed assignment in human history: the birth of his only begotten Son. Jesus' birth was a consummate example of the extraordinary swaddled in the ordinary. God, in his outrageous love, continues to use ordinary people—you and me—to ring in his kingdom today. God chooses and uses people who are willing to be used by him. Whether what we have seems great or small, God makes it much when we let him have his way. He took the loaves and fish from an ordinary little boy and multiplied it to feed over five thousand people. That's what he wants to do with us.

 Thelma Wells

The Spirit of the Sovereign LORD is on me, because the LORD has anointed me to preach good news to the poor. He has sent me to bind up the brokenhearted, to proclaim freedom for the captives and release from darkness for the prisoners, to proclaim the year of the LORD's favor and the day of vengeance of our God, to comfort all who mourn, and provide for those who grieve in Zion — to bestow on them a crown of beauty instead of ashes, the oil of gladness instead of mourning, and a garment of praise instead of a spirit of despair. They will be called oaks of righteousness, a planting of the LORD for the display of his splendor.

❧Isaiah 61:1–3

*S*alvation by *G*race *T*hrough *J*esus

❦

*W*e are called forth from the darkness to know him who is the light—Jesus. John 8:12 states, "I am the light of the world. Whoever follows me will never walk in darkness, but will have the light of life." And again in John 12:46 Jesus says, "I have come into the world as a light, so that no one who believes in me should stay in darkness."

I have been sprung from the darkness of prison to freedom with him who is the light. He means for me never to walk in darkness again. That should take care of it then; I should experience the freedom of any jailbird recently returned to outside society. The truth is that Christ set me free from the law by fulfilling the law on the cross. That means that what I do and how I serve him is not the ticket to my freedom, nor is it the means by which I impress him or win his love.

Marilyn Meberg

Just as man is destined to die once, and after that to face judgment, so Christ was sacrificed once to take away the sins of many people; and he will appear a second time, not to bear sin, but to bring salvation to those who are waiting for him.

❦Hebrews 9:27:28

It is through the grace of our Lord Jesus that we are saved.

❦Acts 15:11

The Mighty One has done great things for me—holy is his name.

❦Luke 1:49

Who is a God like you, who pardons sin and forgives the transgression of the remnant of his inheritance? You do not stay angry forever but delight to show mercy.

❦Micah 7:18

Theologians use big words to describe God's unique qualities: transcendence, omnipotence, omnipresence. Micah marveled even more over this: God's forgiveness. Unlike the angry gods of other nations, Israel's God delighted to show mercy.

❦NIV Study Bible

Grace

*J*esus Christ offers all of us a sustaining hope in the midst of the here and now. Hope is a heartfelt assurance that our heavenly Father knows what's best for us and never makes a mistake. Joy and fulfillment are not in another town, another job, another life. They're in your very own heart. Believe it. Clasp his hand and come.

You're never too old to start living fully. Ask God for a fresh perspective on your life. Try things you've never tried before. Ask yourself what you want most from life, and go for it.

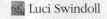 Luci Swindoll

*J*esus was the grace-bearer walking down everyday roads and meeting people where they lived. Like the Samaritan woman, it is never too late and we are never too lost to be found by God's grace through Jesus:

When a Samaritan woman came to draw water, Jesus said to her, "Will you give me a drink?" . . .The Samaritan woman said to him, "You are a Jew and I am a Samaritan woman. How can you ask me for a drink?" (For Jews do not associate with Samaritans.) Jesus answered her, "If you knew the gift of God and who it is that asks you for a drink, you would have asked him and he would have given you living water."

"Sir," the woman said, "you have nothing to draw with and the well is deep. Where can you get this living water? . . . Jesus answered, "Everyone who drinks this water will be thirsty again, but whoever drinks the water I give him will never thirst. Indeed, the water I give him will become in him a spring of water welling up to eternal life."

ℚJohn 4:7–14

When we were under the sentence of death, condemned by our sins, Jesus died in our place. By declaring faith in Jesus, we accept his death as an exchange of life— his for ours.

&NIV Christian Growth
Study Bible

The LORD longs to be gracious to you; he rises to show you compassion. . . . Blessed are all who wait for him!

&Isaiah 30:18

The Lord our God is merciful and forgiving, even though we have rebelled against him.

&Daniel 9:9

I have been crucified with Christ and I no longer live, but Christ lives in me. The life I live in the body, I live by faith in the Son of God, who loved me and gave himself for me.

&Galatians 2:20

*T*o be blessed is to discover that God cherishes us more deeply than we do ourselves. This love is so strange and overwhelming that it transforms our lives. It leaves us not as different people, but as our true selves without any of the pretense. Thus, to receive God's blessing is to come home to a place we have never been, but know we belong there the moment we arrive. It is the place where we are unconditionally loved.

The word for blessing in the Hebrew is ashir. It means to find the right path. After spending a lot of time on the wrong paths, you know that the right one would lead you to this God who cherishes you. When Jesus used the word blessed in the Beatitudes he claimed that the right path was the opposite one from what you expected. "Blessed are the poor in spirit, for theirs is the kingdom of heaven . . . Blessed are the meek for they will inherit the earth" (Matthew 5:3,5). He could also have said, "Blessed are the receivers, for they know they are cherished." The right path isn't the road that we climb up. It is the road that God climbs down to bless us.

M. Craig Barnes

*W*hat a lavish God we serve. His expressions of love and commitment to us are limitless. He keeps every promise he makes. His giving is never-ending—an eternal fountain, flowing forever. His life pours into us as we open ourselves to him. His love is unconditional. Faithful.

Know how much he loves you this day. Don't mistake your ability to love or understand with his ability to love and understand. I suppose if you told Jesus, "I love you all the way" he would answer back that he loved you all the way to the cross—and that he'll continue to love you throughout eternity. It takes your breath away, and you can only respond with a heart of thankfulness.

Kathy Troccoli

The LORD *was gracious to them and had compassion and showed concern for them because of his covenant.*

❧2 Kings 13:23

For I am convinced that neither death nor life, neither angels nor demons, neither the present nor the future, nor any powers, neither height nor depth, nor anything else in all creation, will be able to separate us from the love of God that is in Christ Jesus our Lord.

❧Romans 8:38–39

He redeemed my soul from going down to the pit, and I will live to enjoy the light.

❧Job 33:28

Is the God of the Old Testament different from the God of the New Testament? The Old Testament shows us a God of judgment, while the New Testament reveals a God of grace. Yet here in Job, one of the oldest books of the Bible, God's grace shines clearly. God has always been gracious, and he always will be.

❧NIV Collegiate Devotional Bible

Grace

The Lord opens his arms wide to the
poor, the sick, the ugly, the lonely, the weak,
the ungifted, the unlovely, the unlikely. That's
because of his great love. It's also because
what's in a person's heart matters more to
him than what's on the outside.

 Joni Eareckson Tada

How can I repay the LORD
  for all his goodness to me?
I will lift up the cup of salvation
  and call on the name of the LORD.
I will fulfill my vows to the LORD
  in the presence of all his people.

Psalm 116:12–14

In his love and mercy he redeemed them; he lifted them up and carried them all the days of old.

       ❦Isaiah 63:9

The LORD has heard my cry for mercy; the LORD accepts my prayer.

       ❦Psalm 6:9

Seek good, not evil, that you may live. Then the LORD God Almighty will be with you, just as you say he is.

       ❦Amos 5:14

If you're a seeker, realize that God desires for you to follow him in every area of your life. Don't be like those people who let God affect some areas of their lives but close him out of others.

       ❦The Journey NIV,
          A Bible for Seekers

Grace in Times of Trouble

There is a spiritual realm where you can know God, where you are known and loved for who you are, where the garbage surrounding you doesn't obscure the beauty God sees in you. There God will free you from the bondage of your present condition and give you his power to change. He alone can see past the garbage to the woman you can become.

While your life story is unique, there are longings of the heart that seem to be universal: the desire to find true love, the desire that someone will affirm our inherent value regardless of our situation, the hope that we can change. God finds each of us in the cinders of a less than perfect world, held back from the life we dream of living. He longs to raise us up to a high position, transform us, and grant us his power, so he seeks us out, inviting each of us to dance with him.

Connie Neal

*Answer me, O LORD, out of the goodness
of your love;
    in your great mercy turn to me.
Do not hide your face from your servant;
    answer me quickly, for I am in trouble.
Come near and rescue me.*

> ॐPsalm 69:16–18

*Jesus said, "I have told you these things, so
that in me you may have peace. In this world
you will have trouble. But take heart! I have
overcome the world."*

> ॐJohn 16:33

*Praise be to the God and Father of our Lord
Jesus Christ, the Father of compassion and the
God of all comfort, who comforts us in all our
troubles, so that we can comfort those in any
trouble with the comfort we ourselves have
received from God.*

> ॐ2 Corinthians 1:4

*G*od knows where you are and what you've been through—it is that very thing that he will use to "save some." He wants to use you—warts and all—because you are uniquely his and uniquely placed right where he needs you to be. We are one body with many parts. God has ordained your life and circumstances to minister hope to someone walking the same path you have been down before. You see, God can use anything in our background to minister his grace to us and through us.

Chonda Pierce

For nothing is impossible with God.

    ❧Luke 1:37

In him we have redemption through his blood, the forgiveness of sins, in accordance with the riches of God's grace

    ❧Ephesians 1:7

O LORD, truly I am your servant; I am your servant, the son of your maidservant you have freed me from my chains. I will sacrifice a thank offering to you and call on the name of the LORD.
I will fulfill my vows to the LORD in the presence of all his people, in the courts of the house of the LORD—in your midst, O Jerusalem. Praise the LORD.

    ❧Psalm 116:16–19

Grace

Often, we must allow the softening mulch of God's forgiveness to give air and breath to the soil of our hearts. Prejudices must be released. Fear must be replaced by trust, and suspicion by childlike hope and acceptance.

Sue Benson

To him who is able to keep you from falling and to present you before his glorious presence without fault and with great joy—to the only God our Savior be glory, majesty, power and authority, through Jesus Christ our Lord, before all ages, now and forevermore! Amen.

Jude 24–25

Grace and peace to you from God our Father and the Lord Jesus Christ. Praise be to the God and Father of our Lord Jesus Christ, the Father of compassion and the God of all comfort, who comforts us in all our troubles, so that we can comfort those in any trouble with the comfort we ourselves have received from God. For just as the sufferings of Christ flow over into our lives, so also through Christ our comfort overflows. If we are distressed, it is for your comfort and salvation; if we are comforted, it is for your comfort, which produces in you patient endurance of the same sufferings we suffer. And our hope for you is firm, because we know that just as you share in our sufferings, so also you share in our comfort.

❧2 Corinthians 1:1–7

*N*ot only is God the God of peace, but he is also the God of comfort. Jesus Christ suffered greatly and unjustly when he went to the cross. He fully understands and identifies with our suffering, and he knows the kind of comfort we need.

❧NIV Spiritual Formation Bible

If we have ears to hear, God will surely speak to us, and sometimes he will even use an angel to tell us of his mercy and guide us along the way.

Ann Spangler

He makes his angels winds, his servants flames of fire.

Hebrews 1:7

And there were shepherds living out in the fields nearby, keeping watch over their flocks at night. An angel of the Lord appeared to them, and the glory of the Lord shone around them, and they were terrified. But the angel said to them, "Do not be afraid. I bring you good news of great joy that will be for all the people. Today in the town of David a Savior has been born to you; he is Christ the Lord. This will be a sign to you: You will find a baby wrapped in cloths and lying in a manger."

Luke 2:8–12

Jesus said, "Do not look down on one of these little ones. For I tell you that their angels in heaven always see the face of my Father."

Matthew 18:10

When we grasp God's eternal view of the incidents in our lives, we can be thankful for all things—even for the difficult experiences that wouldn't commonly be thought of as "blessings."

Today a speeding delivery truck driver ran over some of my flowers and knocked down the little garden wall that my husband so lovingly built last year—again! When I got through shaking my head over the damage, I opened the package he had left and found a nice surprise—a lovely present from a friend I hadn't seen in months. The incident made me realize that I sometimes receive God's gifts in the same way. Seemingly pointless problems that pop up in my path may deliver a packet of grace if I'm willing to stop wailing and open it!

Pat Matuszak

God gives grace to the humble.

꙳Proverbs 3:34

Do not forsake wisdom, and she will protect you; love her, and she will watch over you. . . . Esteem her, and she will exalt you; embrace her, and she will honor you. She will set a garland of grace on your head and present you with a crown of splendor.

꙳Proverbs 4:6–9

The following story was related by Mrs. Charles H. Spurgeon, who suffered with poor health for more than twenty-five years:

At the end of a dull and dreary day, I lay resting on my couch as the night grew darker. Although my room was bright and cozy, some of the darkness outside seemed to have entered my soul and obscured its spiritual vision.

With a sorrowful heart I asked, "Why does the Lord deal with a child of his in this way?" Suddenly I heard a sweet, soft sound like the tender trill of a robin beneath my window. I asked aloud, "What can that be? Surely no bird can be singing outside at this time of year or night."

Then my friend exclaimed, "It's coming from the log on the fire!" The fire was unshackling the imprisoned music from deep within the old oak's heart! Perhaps the oak had acquired this song during the days when all was well with him—when birds sang merrily on his branches, and while the soft sunlight streaked his tender leaves with gold. The intense heat of the fire wrenched from him both a song and a sacrifice at once. Then I realized: when the fires of affliction draw songs of praise from us, we are indeed purified and our God is glorified.

Yes, singing in the fire! God helping us, sometimes using the only way he can to get harmony from our hard and apathetic hearts.

Mrs. Charles Spurgeon

*P*eople who are God's without reservation "have learned to be content whatever the circumstances." His will becomes their will, and they desire to do for him whatever he desires them to do. They strip themselves of everything, and in their nakedness find everything restored hundredfold.

> The clouds of trials, bearing burdens rare,
> Leave in the soul, a moisture settled deep:
> Life stirs by the powerful law of God;
> And where before the thirsty camel trod,
> There the richest beauties to life's land-
> scape leap.
> Then read in cloud that comes to you
> The words of Paul, in letters large and
> clear:
> So will those clouds your soul with bless-
> ings feed,
> And with a constant trust as you do read,
> All things together work for good. Fret not,
> nor fear!

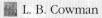 L. B. Cowman

Grace

*I cry out to God Most High, to God, who
fulfills his purpose for me.
He sends from heaven and saves me, rebuking
those who hotly pursue me;
God sends his love and his faithfulness. . . .
My heart is steadfast, O God, my heart is
steadfast;
I will sing and make music.
For great is your love, reaching to the heavens;
your faithfulness reaches to the skies.
Be exalted, O God, above the heavens;
let your glory be over all the earth.*

෨Psalm 57:1–3,7, 10–11

*You know the grace of our Lord Jesus Christ,
that though he was rich, yet for your sakes he
became poor, so that you through his poverty
might become rich.*

෨2 Corinthians 8:9

*I will give thanks to the LORD because of his
righteousness and will sing praise to the name
of the LORD Most High.*

෨Psalm 7:17

The good things here in this life are merely images of the better things we will know in heaven. It's like the artwork I produce. I draw scenes from nature around me, but those drawings are only a feeble, sketchy attempt to mirror what I see. I imitate with a gray pencil what God has painted with an infinite array of colors. My drawings, bounded by the edges of a sketch pad, can never fully portray God's boundless nature above, beneath, and around us. Just as my artwork pleasantly but imperfectly reflects the nature I see, so this earth that we know is only a preliminary sketch of the glory that will one day be revealed. Reality—the final painting—lies in heaven.

Joni Eareckson Tada

How brightly beams the morning star!
What sudden radiance from afar
            Doth glad us with its shining?
Brightness of God, that breaks our night
And fills the darkened souls with light
            Who long for truth were pining!
                    Rightly leads us,
                    Life bestowing.
Praise, O praise such love o'erflowing!

Through thee alone can we be blest;
Then deep be on our hearts imprest
            The love that thou hast borne us;
So make us ready to fulfil
With ardent zeal thy holy will,
            Though men may vex or scorn us;
Hold us, fold us, lest we fail thee.
                    Lo, we hail thee,
                    Long to know thee!
All we are and have we owe thee.

J. A. Schlegel

Grace

*G*od let me walk to a place where I realized that no one loved me as he did. In his great wisdom, he let me realize that nowhere else in the whole wide world, nowhere in all creation, can I go from his presence. He wouldn't let me go.

All this time I thought I was holding on to God, grasping with all my earthly might not to let go. And that is precisely why God told me to let go. He knew that when I finally loosened by grip, I would realize he was holding me fast.

God's Word and his promises began to sink in. I realized, I really do believe this! And for the first time in months, I felt a glimmering of hope.

Jan Dravecky

. . .The Lord your God is gracious and compassionate. He will not turn his face from you if you return to him.

&2 Chronicles 30:9

O Love that wilt not let me go,
I rest my weary soul in Thee;
I give Thee back the life I owe,
That in Thine ocean depths its flow
May richer, fuller be.

O Light that foll'west all my way,
I yield my flick'ring torch to Thee;
My heart restores its borrowed ray,
That in Thy sunshine's glow its day
May brighter, fairer be.

O Joy that seekest me thro' pain,
I cannot close my heart to Thee;
I trace the rainbow thro' the rain,
And feel the promise is not vain
That morn shall tearless be.

O Cross that liftest up my head,
I dare not ask to hide from Thee;
I lay in dust life's glory dead,
And from the ground there blossoms red,
Life that shall endless be.

George Matheson

Where can I go from your Spirit? Where can I flee from your presence?

If I go up to the heavens, you are there; if I make my bed in the depths, you are there.

If I rise on the wings of the dawn, if I settle on the far side of the sea,

even there your hand will guide me, your right hand will hold me fast.

If I say, "Surely the darkness will hide me and the light become night around me," even the darkness will not be dark to you; the night will shine like the day, for darkness is as light to you.

For you created my inmost being; you knit me together in my mother's womb.

I praise you because I am fearfully and wonderfully made; your works are wonderful, I know that full well.

My frame was not hidden from you when I was made in the secret place. When I was woven together in the depths of the earth, your eyes saw my unformed body. All the days ordained for me were written in your book before one of them came to be.

Psalm 139:7–16

The soul is immortal and must survive all time, even to eternity. . . . The infinite goodness of God, who delighteth that his mercy should triumph over his justice, would not suffer the whole race of mankind to be ruined and destroyed . . . he laid help upon one that is mighty, that is able and willing to save to the uttermost all such as shall come unto God through him.

This Saviour was that seed of the woman, that was promised should bruise the head of the serpent, break the power of the devil, and bring mankind again into savable condition. And upon a view of that satisfaction which Christ would make for the sins of the whole world was the penalty of Adam's disobedience suspended . . . and God renewed his covenant with man, not on the former condition of perfect obedience, but on condition of faith in Christ Jesus.

Susanna Wesley

God has saved us and called us. . .not because of anything we have done but because of his own purpose and grace. This grace was given us in Christ Jesus before the beginning of time, but it has now been revealed through the appearing of our Savior, Christ Jesus, who has destroyed death and has brought life and immortality to light through the gospel.

❧2 Timothy 1:9–10

How precious to me are your thoughts, O God! How vast is the sum of them! Were I to count them, they would outnumber the grains of sand. When I awake, I am still with you.

❧Psalm 139:17–18

Grace

_H_ope is a heartfelt assurance that our heavenly Father knows what's best for us and never makes a mistake. God's says, "Trust me. Remember my Word. Believe . . . and wait."

Of course, our greatest hope lies waiting for us at the end of time, when all God's purposes will be fulfilled. We will go to live with Jesus Christ, who by his grace redeemed us, loved us through our trials, provided joy in the midst of heartache, peace for our troubled hearts, and freedom from a boring lifestyle. We'll be with him forever—an outrageous reality!

 Luci Swindoll

Your word, O LORD, is eternal;
it stands firm in the heavens.
Your faithfulness continues through all
generations;
you established the earth, and it endures.
Your laws endure to this day,
for all things serve you.
If your law had not been my delight,
I would have perished in my affliction.
I will never forget your precepts,
for by them you have preserved my life.

୫Psalm 119:89–93

But when the kindness and love of God our
Savior appeared, he saved us, not because of
righteous things we had done, but because of
his mercy. He saved us through the washing of
rebirth and renewal by the Holy Spirit, whom
he poured out on us generously through Jesus
Christ our Savior, so that, having been justified
by his grace, we might become heirs having the
hope of eternal life. This is a trustworthy saying.
And I want you to stress these things, so that
those who have trusted in God may be careful
to devote themselves to doing what is good.
These things are excellent and profitable for
everyone.

୫Titus 3:4–8

Eternal Life

❧

*J*esus, though sinless, bore our sins. Coming into a relationship with Christ is not just an intellectual exercise; it is a personal encounter. Through faith we accept that a perfect God allowed his son to endure agony and death on our behalf. This concept often motivates me: being forgiven for so much causes me to love much!

Jesus came into the world through a miracle—the miracle of the virgin birth. And his death sets the stage for the greatest miracle of all: his resurrection! Knowing about his death is key to understanding God's sacrifice on our behalf. We receive pardon for our sin as a result of accepting his death in our place. This supernatural event conveys the power of God and is one of the main events that makes Christianity unique. Jesus ascended into heaven and lives today. Because he lives, he empowers us with his Holy Spirit.

Becky Tirabassi

Grace

And I heard a loud voice from the throne saying, "Now the dwelling of God is with men, and he will live with them. They will be his people, and God himself will be with them and be their God. He will wipe every tear from their eyes. There will be no more death or mourning or crying or pain, for the old order of things has passed away."

He who was seated on the throne said, "I am making everything new!" Then he said, "Write this down, for these words are trustworthy and true."

He said to me: "It is done. I am the Alpha and the Omega, the Beginning and the End. To him who is thirsty I will give to drink without cost from the spring of the water of life. He who overcomes will inherit all this, and I will be his God and he will be my son."

ॐRevelation 21:3–7

*O*ur best foot forward is the step we make toward the cross. Eternal life is a gift from God that we cannot procure through good works. God alone is good and bestows his goodness to those who realize they cannot measure up to God's standards and who receive the gift of salvation through faith in Christ. We can't make it to heaven or know God even when we consistently put our best foot forward. We are incapable of relating to God apart from faith in Christ's death, burial, and resurrection. We certainly can inherit eternal life, but only through faith in Christ's effort on the cross, not ours. There are many very good men and women as we define good, but they can never be good enough to attain to the flawless righteousness of God. "There is no one righteous [good enough], not even one," Paul quoted the psalmist in his letter to the Romans (3:10).

Charles Stanley

May our Lord Jesus Christ himself and God our Father, who loved us and by his grace gave us eternal encouragement and good hope, encourage your hearts and strengthen you.

❧ 2 Thessalonians 2:16–17

If only for this life we have hope in Christ, we are to be pitied more than all men. But Christ has indeed been raised from the dead, the firstfruits of those who have fallen asleep. For since death came through a man, the resurrection of the dead comes also through a man. For as in Adam all die, so in Christ all will be made alive.

❧ 1 Corinthians 15:19–22

Listen, I tell you a mystery: We will not all sleep, but we will all be changed—in a flash, in the twinkling of an eye, at the last trumpet. For the trumpet will sound, the dead will be raised imperishable, and we will be changed. For the perishable must clothe itself with the imperishable, and the mortal with immortality. When the perishable has been clothed with the imperishable, and the mortal with immortality, then the saying that is written will come true: "Death has been swallowed up in victory." "Where, O death, is your victory? Where, O death, is your sting?"

❧ 1 Corinthians 15:51–55

We believe that Jesus died and rose again and so we believe that God will bring with Jesus those who have fallen asleep in him. According to the Lord's own word, we tell you that we who are still alive, who are left till the coming of the Lord, will certainly not precede those who have fallen asleep. For the Lord himself will come down from heaven, with a loud command, with the voice of the archangel and with the trumpet call of God, and the dead in Christ will rise first. After that, we who are still alive and are left will be caught up together with them in the clouds to meet the Lord in the air. And so we will be with the Lord forever.

❧1 Thessalonians 4:14–18

If my people, who are called by my name, will humble themselves and pray and seek my face and turn from their wicked ways, then will I hear from heaven and will forgive their sin.

❧2 Chronicles 7:14

There's a sweet and blessed story
Of the Christ Who came from glory
Just to rescue me from sin and misery.
He in lovingkindness sought me,
And from and sin shame hath brought me.
Hallelujah! Jesus ransomed me.

From the depth of sin and sadness
To the heights of joy and gladness
Jesus lifted me, in mercy full and free.
With His precious blood He bought me;
When I knew Him not, He sought me,
And in love divine He ransomed me.

By and by with joy increasing,
And with gratitude unceasing,
Lifted up with Christ forevermore to be,
I will join the hosts there singing,
In the anthem ever ringing,
To the King of Love, Who ransomed me.

 Julia Johnston

*L*ord Jesus, I've been working myself to death to get to you. Now I know I don't have to put forth one ounce of strength; I only need to cry out to you—the Son of God—who died on a cross for me. You endured the pain of all my sins and rose victoriously, fully alive once again. I accept your finished work and your offer of salvation now.

Amen.

A Prayer by
Charles Stanley

Grace
Gives Us...

Holiness

❧

*I*nside the wrapping around the idea and the word grace we find the beautiful qualities of the gift God gave to all his children. As his own beloved family we share in the activities and values that are closest to his heart. Our Father is a holy, courageous leader with strong purpose and direction. He fulfills his promises to provide for all our needs and bring healing to this broken world through his grace.

I have a choice about how to respond to those who mistreat me. God has given me outrageous freedom; I'm free at any time to hurl stones of condemnation at the sinners around me. . . just as soon as I become sinless myself.

Barbara Johnson

We are God's workmanship, created in Christ Jesus to do good works, which God prepared in advance for us to do.

❧Ephesians 2:10

God did not call us to be impure, but to live a holy life.

❧1 Thessalonians 4:7

What does the LORD your God ask of you but to fear the LORD your God, to walk in all his ways, to love him, to serve the LORD your God with all your heart and with all your soul.

❧Deuteronomy 10:12

Serve him with wholehearted devotion and with a willing mind, for the LORD searches every heart and understands every motive behind the thoughts. If you seek him, he will be found by you.

❧1 Chronicles 28:9

"*Waywardness*" is something God means to redirect and heal. God loves us too much to leave us muddling about in our sin. No matter what our problem—lying, cheating, marital unfaithfulness, yelling at the kids, fudging on the income tax, bitterness, anger, gossip, etc., etc.—God is tenacious in his commitment to developing us into people of integrity who love him, reflect him to others, and delight in doing his will.

In the midst of our stumbling, wayward humanity, God "loves us freely." Abundantly. Outrageously.

Now I don't know about you, but that promise is so mind-bogglingly gracious that I could almost volunteer to walk the high wire! God is not saying he'll just look the other way when he see "waywardness"; he loves us too much not to deal with our rebellious nature. But even when we least deserve it, he loves us without restraint.

Marilyn Meberg

Thou hidden love of God, whose height,
> Whose depth unfathom'd no man knows,
I see from far thy beauteous light,
> Only I sigh for thy repose;
My heart is pain'd, nor can it be
> At rest, till it finds rest in thee.
Yet hindrances strew all the way;
> I aim at thee, yet from thee stray.
'Tis mercy all, that thou hast brought
> My mind to seek her peace in thee.

John Wesley

Search me, O God, and know my heart; test me and know my anxious thoughts. See if there is any offensive way in me, and lead me in the way everlasting.

Psalm 139:23–24

Therefore, since we are surrounded by such a great cloud of witnesses, let us throw off everything that hinders and the sin that so easily entangles, and let us run with perseverance the race marked out for us. Let us fix our eyes on Jesus, the author and perfecter of our faith, who for the joy set before him endured the cross, scorning its shame, and sat down at the right hand of the throne of God. Consider him who endured such opposition from sinful men, so that you will not grow weary and lose heart.

Hebrews 12:1–3

We see Jesus, who was made a little lower than the angels, now crowned with glory and honor because he suffered death, so that by the grace of God he might taste death for everyone.

Therefore, since we have a great high priest who has gone through the heavens, Jesus the Son of God, let us hold firmly to the faith we profess. For we do not have a high priest who is unable to sympathize with our weaknesses, but we have one who has been tempted in every way, just as we are—yet was without sin.

$\mathcal{L}$et us then approach the throne of grace with confidence, so that we may receive mercy and find grace to help us in our time of need.

We have this hope as an anchor for the soul, firm and secure.

Let us hold unswervingly to the hope we profess, for he who promised is faithful. And let us consider how we may spur one another on toward love and good deeds. Let us not give up meeting together, as some are in the habit of doing, but let us encourage one another—and all the more as you see the Day approaching.

Hebrews 2:9; 4:14, 16; 6:19; 10:23–25

Phoebe Palmer, often referred to as the "Mother of the Holiness Movement," was the most influential woman in nineteenth-century Methodism. She lived in New York City with her husband, a physician, and began her ministry in the 1830s with her Tuesday Meeting for the Promotion of Holiness, which she continued for some twenty years. These were very significant meetings. The well-publicized success of her informal prayer meetings inspired other women to conduct the same type of ministry, and dozens of such meetings sprang up all over the country, bringing together Christians from all denominations. In 1858 Walter Palmer, Phoebe's husband, purchased the "Guide to Holiness" magazine and under Phoebe's editorship the circulation grew from thirteen thousand subscriptions to thirty thousand. Besides her editing duties, Phoebe traveled with her husband, conducting evangelistic meetings. There was a very practical side to her concept of Christianity, and she played an influential role in establishing the Hedding Church, a New York city mission, and founded Five Points Mission.

Ruth Tucker

*G*ospel holiness is that state which is attained by the believer when, through faith in the infinite merit of the Saviour, body and soul are ceaselessly presented as a living sacrifice to God. The purpose of the soul is steadily bent to know nothing among men, save Christ and Him crucified, and the eye of faith is fixed on "the Lamb of God which taketh away the sin of the world."

Holiness implies salvation from sin, a redemption from all iniquity. The soul, through faith, being laid upon the altar that sanctifies the gift, experiences, constantly the all-cleansing blood of Jesus. Through this it knows the blessedness of being presented faultless before the throne.
In order to be continually washed, cleansed, and renewed after the image of God, our sacrifice must be ceaselessly presented. This is implied in the expression, "a living sacrifice."

Phoebe Palmer, 1845

Strength When Tempted

❧

I knew from God's Word that I had a choice about how to respond. I knew I could use my freedom to hate or to love. God himself showed me how to choose love: "When someone gives you a hard time, respond with the energies of prayer, for then you are working out of your true selves, your God-created selves" (Matthew 5:44, *The Message*).

🦋 Thelma Wells

Be strong in the grace that is in Christ Jesus.

❧2 Timothy 2:1

How much better to get wisdom than gold, to choose understanding rather than silver!

❧Proverbs 16:16

*N*ot to us, O Lord, not to us but to your name be the glory, because of your love and faithfulness. Why do the nations say, "Where is their God?" Our God is in heaven; he does whatever pleases him. But their idols are silver and gold, made by the hands of men. They have mouths, but cannot speak, eyes, but they cannot see; they have ears, but cannot hear, noses, but they cannot smell; they have hands, but cannot feel, feet, but they cannot walk; nor can they utter a sound with their throats. Those who make them will be like them, and so will all who trust in them.

❧Psalms 115:1–8

*S*ometimes we look for help in places where it will never be found. If we ask God for help, all of these other resources are useless— they are only human inventions. God alone knows what we need and has the power to fill our lives with meaning and joy.

❧NIV Spiritual Formation Bible

Show me your ways, O LORD, teach me
your paths; guide me in your truth and teach
me, for you are God my Savior, and my hope
is in you all day long.
Remember, O LORD, your great mercy and love,
for they are from of old.
Remember not the sins of my youth and my
rebellious ways; according to your love remember
me, for you are good, O LORD.
Good and upright is the LORD; therefore he
instructs sinners in his ways.
He guides the humble in what is right and
teaches them his way.
All the ways of the LORD are loving and faithful
for those who keep the demands of his
covenant.

❧Psalm 25:4–10

Come, let us bow down in worship,
let us kneel before the LORD our Maker;
for he is our God
and we are the people of his pasture,
the flock under his care.

❧Psalm 95:6–7

God has said, "Never will I leave you; never will I forsake you." So we say with confidence, "The Lord is my helper; I will not be afraid. What can man do to me?" Remember your leaders, who spoke the word of God to you. Consider the outcome of their way of life and imitate their faith. Jesus Christ is the same yesterday and today and forever.

❧Hebrews 13:5–8

O LORD; may your love and your truth always protect me.

❧Psalm 40:11

In your hands are strength and power to exalt and give strength to all. Now, our God, we give you thanks, and praise your glorious name.

❧1 Chronicles 29:12–13

You are awesome, O God, in your sanctuary; the God of Israel gives power and strength to his people. Praise be to God!

❧Psalm 68:35

*G*race gave me the courage to face my biggest fears and the harshest truths about my life because it held onto me and never let go. I felt an overwhelming thankfulness deep in my bones. I knew I could never pay for this awesome gift, but it had my name on it, and it would never be taken away.

Sheila Walsh

*S*o then, just as you have received Christ Jesus as Lord, continue to live in him, rooted and built up in him, strengthened in the faith as you were taught.

Colossians 2:6–7

*T*he Spirit helps us in our weakness. We do not know what we ought to pray for, but the Spirit himself intercedes for us with groans that words cannot express.

Romans 8:26

*The LORD is my shepherd, I shall not
be in want.
He makes me lie down in green pastures,
he leads me beside quiet waters,
he restores my soul.
He guides me in paths of righteousness for his
name's sake.
Even though I walk through the valley of the
shadow of death,
I will fear no evil, for you are with me;
your rod and your staff, they comfort me.
You prepare a table before me in the presence of
my enemies.
You anoint my head with oil; my cup overflows.
Surely goodness and love will follow me all the
days of my life,
and I will dwell in the house of the LORD forever.*

❧Psalm 23

Grace Gives Us

This unmerited favor from God not only secures our eternal salvation, but it also empowers us to keep walking steadily through life's trials and torments. Because we have received "so great a Grace," our lives are altogether different. We have the ability to live on a different plane. Different values and standards for behavior guide us. It's all wrapped up in the word abundance. No longer do we merely survive, but we live fully; no longer endure but enjoy; no longer walk a tightrope but relax completely. God's outrageous grace has given us an abundant life.

Luci Swindoll

Dear friends, now we are children of God, and what we will be has not yet been made known. But we know that when he appears, we shall be like him, for we shall see him as he is.

1 John 3:2

We have all had human fathers who disciplined us and we respected them for it. How much more should we submit to the Father of our spirits and live! Our fathers disciplined us for a little while as they thought best; but God disciplines us for our good, that we may share in his holiness. No discipline seems pleasant at the time, but painful. Later on, however, it produces a harvest of righteousness and peace for those who have been trained by it. Therefore, strengthen your feeble arms and weak knees. "Make level paths for your feet," so that the lame may not be disabled, but rather healed. Make every effort to live in peace with all men and to be holy; without holiness no one will see the Lord. See to it that no one misses the grace of God and that no bitter root grows up to cause trouble and defile many.

༜Hebrews 12:9–15

*J*esus, your light of love we see
    In the midst of a world that's falling.
Light of the world, set us free;
    With our hearts we hear your calling;
You are all we need.

Light of Love shine now!
    Let God's glory be our way.
In our hearts show us how
    Grace is the sun of our new day.
The Lamb will be our light!

When we come to Your loving arms,
    Leave the shadows of night behind,
You free us from hatred's harm;
    We find rest in our Father kind.
You are all we need.

Pat Matuszak

*Create in me a pure heart,
O God, and renew a steadfast spirit
within me. . . .
Restore to me the joy of your salvation
and grant me a willing spirit, to
sustain me.
Then I will teach transgressors your ways,
and sinners will turn back to you. . . .
and my tongue will sing of your
righteousness.
O Lord, open my lips,
and my mouth will declare your praise.*

◦ Psalm 51:10–15

*You have come to Mount Zion, to the
heavenly Jerusalem, the city of the living
God. You have come to thousands upon
thousands of angels in joyful assembly, to
the church of the firstborn, whose names
are written in heaven. You have come to
God, the judge of all men, to the spirits of
righteous men made perfect, to Jesus the
mediator of a new covenant.*

◦ Hebrews 12:22–24

Glimpsing God's heart makes me want to do back flips while swinging from a trapeze. Trust me, these are not natural feelings for this clown! But then, God's love is not a natural love. Instead, the Lord's supernatural nature allows us to do things way outside our comfort zone—like love the unlovely, which was what Christ did when he died for us. Now we are called to live lovingly for him.

Patsy Clairmont

But because of his great love for us, God, who is rich in mercy, made us alive with Christ even when we were dead in transgressions—it is by grace you have been saved.

Ephesians 2:4–5

Thou walkest with me when I walk;
When to my bed for rest I go,
I find thee there,
And everywhere.

Mary Herbert

You hem me in —behind and before;
you have laid your hand upon me.
Such knowledge is too wonderful for me,
too lofty for me to attain.

⮑Psalm 139:5–6

May the Lord direct your hearts into God's love
and Christ's perseverance.

⮑2 Thessalonians 3:5

And he who searches our hearts knows the mind
of the Spirit, because the Spirit intercedes for the
saints in accordance with God's will.
We know that in all things God works for the good of
those who love him.

⮑Romans 8:27–28

Those who belong to Christ Jesus have crucified the
sinful nature with its passions and desires. Since we
live by the Spirit, let us keep in step with the Spirit.

⮑Galatians 5:24–25

Purpose for *Living*

༙

*W*hat an incredible paradox I live in. To understand who I am without God and what I'm capable of without Jesus is so sobering. I'm easily subject to passions, lusts, lies, idols, sin, and death. At the same time, I know who I am in Jesus: a conqueror, a child of God, a sinner saved by grace, a receiver of the gift of heaven.

Kathy Troccoli

How great is the love the Father has lavished on us, that we should be called children of God! And that is what we are! The reason the world does not know us is that it did not know him.

❧1 John 3:1

I have raised you up for this very purpose, that I might show you my power and that my name might be proclaimed in all the earth.

❧Exodus 9:16

To God belong wisdom and power; counsel and understanding are his.

❧Job 12:13

He has made everything beautiful in its time.

❧Ecclesiastes 3:11

I pray that out of his glorious riches God may strengthen you with power through his Spirit in your inner being, so that Christ may dwell in your hearts through faith. And I pray that you, being rooted and established in love, may have power, together with all the saints, to grasp how wide and long and high and deep is the love of Christ.

❧Ephesians 3:16–18

*A*bigail is "a woman of good understanding, and of a beautiful countenance." In her, winsomeness and wisdom were wed. She had brains as well as beauty. A beautiful woman with a beautiful mind as she had is surely one of God's masterpieces. She experienced that in God there was a source of joy enabling her to be independent of the adverse, trying circumstances of her miserable home life.

Herbert Lockyer

When Abigail saw David, she quickly got off her donkey and bowed down before David with her face to the ground. She fell at his feet and said: "My lord, let the blame be on me alone. Please let your servant speak to you; hear what your servant has to say. May my lord pay no attention to that wicked man Nabal. He is just like his name—his name is Fool, and folly goes with him. But as for me, your servant, I did not see the men my master sent. . . . let this gift, which your servant has brought to my master, be given to the men who follow you. Please forgive your servant's offense. . . .

David said to Abigail, "Praise be to the LORD, the God of Israel, who has sent you today to meet me. May you be blessed for your good judgment and for keeping me from bloodshed this day and from avenging myself with my own hands." Then David accepted from her hand what she had brought him and said, "Go home in peace. I have heard your words and granted your request."

1 Samuel 25:23–25, 27–28, 32–33, 35

I don't recall a time when I didn't love the Lord and want to serve him. I don't say that to sound pious or self-righteous, it's just the truth. I rebelled as a teen against parental strictures and traditional structures, but I never rebelled against God.

There have been times when I thought I was lacking something because I had no dazzling experience to relate. But over the years I've come to realize the value of my quiet sort of experience.

And even though there haven't been blinding visions or bright lights, there have been times of definite comfort and guidance from God. Like when he spoke to me from Isaiah as a teenager, reassuring me that I wasn't a nobody:

Fear not, for I have redeemed you; I have summoned you by name; you are mine (Isaiah 43:1).

Jean Syswerda

*Jesus began to teach them, saying:
"Blessed are the poor in spirit, for theirs is
the kingdom of heaven.
Blessed are those who mourn, for they will
be comforted.
Blessed are the meek, for they will inherit the
earth.
Blessed are those who hunger and thirst for
righteousness, for they will be filled.
Blessed are the merciful, for they will be
shown mercy.
Blessed are the pure in heart, for they will
see God.
Blessed are the peacemakers, for they will be
called sons of God."*

Matthew 5:2–9

I thought deeply about what it could mean if Jesus really were alive. I didn't know how he would change my life, but I knew my life needed to change. Perhaps he was the one who saw the real me and would help me become all I longed to be. I prayed, hoping God would hear and let me know these promises were true.

I awoke the next morning with an assurance of love I could neither explain nor deny. It was the assurance that God knew me, saw beyond the garbage, and loved me. Somehow I caught a glimpse of myself as seen through his eyes, and hope began to grow inside me once again. The vision God had of me was far different from what others saw when they looked at me. It was even different from what I saw when I looked at myself. I began to believe in his power to transform me into the woman he had planned for me to become.

When all seemed lost amid fiery trials, the most amazing thing happened. I found a hope in God that was independent of my hopes that he would do a particular thing. I realized that my hope was secure even though life was not. I had to live though those troubles, work through the pressing conflicts with others, grieve my lost dreams, and grow, slowly and painfully, into a more mature woman. But the sense of security I found in God's arms once I considered everything a loss was incredible. In giving up everything, there was nothing left to come between us.

 Connie Neal

Confident Living

৵

The Bible tells us our God is so trustworthy that we are to throw our confidence on him, not leaning on our own limited understanding (Proverbs 3:5). God has already proved how much his love can be trusted by sending Christ to die for us. Wasn't that enough?

Joni Eareckson Tada

The eternal God is your refuge, and underneath are the everlasting arms. . . . Who is like you, a people saved by the LORD? He is your shield and helper and your glorious sword.

৵*Deuteronomy 33:27, 29*

*I will sing of the LORD's great love forever;
with my mouth I will make your faithfulness
known through all generations.
I will declare that your love stands firm
forever,
that you established your faithfulness in
heaven itself. . . .
The heavens praise your wonders, O LORD,
your faithfulness too, in the assembly of the
holy ones.
For who in the skies above can compare
with the LORD?
Who is like the LORD among the heavenly
beings?*

❦Psalm 89:1–2, 5–6

*You will be called by a new name that
the mouth of the LORD will bestow. You will
be a crown of splendor in the LORD's hand,
a royal diadem in the hand of your God.*

❦Isaiah 62:2–3

*You will receive power when the Holy
Spirit comes on you; and you will be my
witnesses in Jerusalem, and in all Judea and
Samaria, and to the ends of the earth.*

❦Acts 1:8

"*Lord*, how can I thank you when I am single and want to be married?"

"Dear God, how can I ever be happy in this dead-end job?"

"God, how can I thank you for broken plumbing in our bathroom when we don't have the money to make repairs?"

How can we have thankful, contented hearts when the circumstances in our lives are not what we had planned and when they lie outside of our control?

God's Word instructs us that God is sovereignly in control, providing for and working out all the circumstances in the lives of those who love him and whom he has called. He is intimately involved with us; he works out his purposes through the events in our lives so that we may be conformed to the image of his Son.

The same God who formed the world in six days knows every hair on our heads. The same God who chose a people for himself before we were born sent his Son to die on the cross to redeem us from our sins.

God's love for his people is not determined by the circumstances in our lives. His love is steadfast. Our marital status, career or finances might fluctuate or totally break apart. In spite of that, however, we can and must give him thanks for his love toward us. We must serve him with unhesitating hearts.

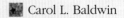 Carol L. Baldwin

*J*oy and confidence will spring up in your heart as you realize that the ultimate supernatural event will be our resurrection to everlasting life with Christ in a place where there will be no more tears, pain, nor tragedy.

See his glory before you! Hear the songs of praises being sung! Hear the great choirs of angels as they sing: "To him who sits on the throne and to the Lamb be praise and honor and glory and power, for ever and ever!" (Revelation 5:13).

Hope MacDonald

*P*raise the Lord, all you nations;
  extol him, all you peoples.
For great is his love toward us,
  and the faithfulness of the Lord
endures forever.

Psalm 117:1–2

Such confidence as this is ours through Christ before God. Not that we are competent in ourselves to claim anything for ourselves, but our competence comes from God.

❧2 Corinthians 3:4–5

In his letters, Paul appears to be a very confident person. However, Paul's confidence is not so much a self-confidence as it is a "God-inspired" confidence. If we trust God to work in and through us, we can be confident that resources are available to overcome any problem we might face.

❧NIV Spiritual Renewal Bible

Trust in the LORD with all your heart and lean not on your own understanding; in all your ways acknowledge him, and he will make your paths straight. Do not be wise in your own eyes; fear the LORD and shun evil. This will bring health to your body and nourishment to your bones.

❧Proverbs 3:5–8

Courage When We Fear

❦

When the Spirit of Christ whispers to your troubled heart, "seek his face," don't delay. This is what is called a prompting or a nudging of the Spirit. He is telling you what to do.

Seek him in his Word and through prayer. The peace that surpasses all understanding will be yours when you hear him whisper, in return, "All is well."

Joni Eareckson Tada

God said, "My grace is sufficient for you, for my power is made perfect in weakness."

❦ 2 Corinthians 12:9

As we face the uncertainties that today may bring, we have the assurance that God knows what we are facing. He is in touch with what is happening to us, and he is concerned.

God is the God of grace and hope. With God's perspective, we can trace his hand on our lives and see that he has transformed the bad things to good, just as he promised he would.

Margaret Fishback
Powers

Do you not know? Have you not heard?
The LORD is the everlasting God,
the Creator of the ends of the earth.
He will not grow tired or weary,
and his understanding no one can fathom.
He gives strength to the weary
and increases the power of the weak.
Even youths grow tired and weary,
and young men stumble and fall;
Those who hope in the LORD
will renew their strength.
They will soar on wings like eagles;
they will run and not grow weary,
they will walk and not be faint.

Isaiah 40:28–31

In the sixth month, God sent the angel Gabriel to Nazareth, a town in Galilee, to a virgin pledged to be married to a man named Joseph, a descendant of David. The virgin's name was Mary.

The angel went to her and said, "Greetings, you who are highly favored! The Lord is with you."

Mary was greatly troubled at his words and wondered what kind of greeting this might be. But the angel said to her, "Do not be afraid, Mary, you have found favor with God. You will be with child and give birth to a son, and you are to give him the name Jesus. He will be great and will be called the Son of the Most High. The Lord God will give him the throne of his father David, and he will reign over the house of Jacob forever; his kingdom will never end."

"How will this be," Mary asked the angel, "since I am a virgin?"

The angel answered, "The Holy Spirit will come upon you, and the power of the Most High will overshadow you. So the holy one to be born will be called the Son of God. Even Elizabeth your relative is going to have a child in her old age, and she who was said to be barren is in her sixth month. For nothing is impossible with God."

"I am the Lord's servant," Mary answered. "May it be to me as you have said." Then the angel left her.

❧Luke 1:26–38

*W*hen I was a young minister's wife and new mother, I suffered from a serious case of low self-image and overcautiousness. Perhaps, more accurately, I could have been called fearful and anxious. It was very difficult for me to speak to a group of more than seven or eight ladies.

As God began to help me with my fearfulness, my own self-image began to improve. Over a period of weeks, and then months, it began to be obvious that God was changing me.

My fears and anxieties were self-imposed. God's choice for me was to have power, love and self-discipline. God did not give me a spirit of fear! My poor self-image, my anxieties, my fears were all my own doing and my sin because I lacked faith to receive those qualities God really wanted me to have.

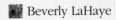 Beverly LaHaye

*S*urely God is my salvation;
I will trust and not be afraid.
The LORD, the LORD, is my strength
and my song;
he has become my salvation.

    ❦Isaiah 12:2

*F*or this reason I remind you to fan
into flame the gift of God, which is in
you . . . For God did not give us a spirit
of timidity, but a spirit of power, of love
and of self-discipline.

    ❦2 Timothy 1:6–7

I will extol the LORD at all times; his
praise will always be on my lips.
My soul will boast in the LORD; let the
afflicted hear and rejoice.
Glorify the LORD with me; let us exalt his
name together.
I sought the LORD, and he answered me;
he delivered me from all my fears.
Those who look to him are radiant; their
faces are never covered with shame.
. . . Taste and see that the LORD is good.

    ❦Psalm 34:1–8

God's Provision for Our Needs

❧

God will send all kinds of blessings. And all his blessings go together like links in a golden chain. If he gives you saving grace, he will also give you comforting grace. God will send "showers of blessings." Look up today, you who are dried and withered plants. Open your leaves and flowers and receive God's heavenly watering.

Charles H. Spurgeon

Surely goodness and love will follow me all the days of my life, and I will dwell in the house of the LORD forever.

❧Psalm 23:6

From the fullness of grace we have all received one blessing after another.

❧John 1:16

The Mighty One has done great things for me— holy is his name. His mercy extends to those who fear him, from generation to generation. He has performed mighty deeds with his arm; he has scattered those who are proud in their inmost thoughts. He has brought down rulers from their thrones but has lifted up the humble. He has filled the hungry with good things but has sent the rich away empty.

❧Luke 1:49–53

Jesus said to them, "I tell you the truth, it is not Moses who has given you the bread from heaven, but it is my Father who gives you the true bread from heaven. For the bread of God is he who comes down from heaven and gives life to the world."

"Sir," they said, "from now on give us this bread."

Then Jesus declared, "I am the bread of life. He who comes to me will never go hungry, and he who believes in me will never be thirsty. But as I told you, you have seen me and still you do not believe. All that the Father gives me will come to me, and whoever comes to me I will never drive away. For I have come down from heaven not to do my will but to do the will of him who sent me."

John 6:32–38

Every good and perfect gift is from above, coming down from the Father of the heavenly lights, who does not change like shifting shadows.

James 1:17

Does Jesus want the best for his children? Sure he does. But that doesn't mean a life of ease and comfort cushioned on a velvet pillow.

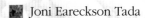 Joni Eareckson Tada

Healing

❧

There are so many potential healing moments in our lives, ministered through the gift of someone's encouraging word or touch, life-changing moments. However all too often we miss them because we fail to stop long enough to hear him speak through the most unlikely servants in the most unlikely places in the most unlikely ways.

Chonda Pierce

The grace of God that brings salvation has appeared to all.

❧Titus 2:11

Give thanks to the LORD, for he is good; his love endures forever.
Let the redeemed of the LORD say this—those he redeemed from the hand of the foe,
those he gathered from the lands, from east and west, from north and south.
Some wandered in desert wastelands, finding no way to a city where they could settle.
They were hungry and thirsty, and their lives ebbed away.
Then they cried out to the LORD in their trouble, and he delivered them from their distress.
He led them by a straight way to a city where they could settle.
Let them give thanks to the LORD for his unfailing love and his wonderful deeds for men,
for he satisfies the thirsty and fills the hungry with good things.

❧Psalm 107:1–9

When I speak of having faith in God, I am not talking about an emotion. Trusting God is not necessarily having trustful feelings. It is an act of the will. Because essentially, trusting God is reasoning with yourself to act upon what you know in your head to be true, even though you do not feel like it is true.

Joni Eareckson Tada

Now I commit you to God and to the word of his grace, which can build you up and give you an inheritance among all those who are sanctified.

Acts 20:32

Thanks be to God for his indescribable gift!

2 Corinthians 9:15

Praise be to the God and Father of our Lord Jesus Christ, who has blessed us in the heavenly realms with every spiritual blessing in Christ.

Ephesians 1:3

How badly do we want to be healed?
For so many years my reluctance to
forgive was like a darkness inside, a
barrier that barred joy and love and so
many good things from my life.
Forgiveness smashed that barrier and has
enabled me to experience the giving and
receiving of love again.

I've seen mankind's idea of justice; I
have more faith in God's. And even God
seems to put a higher priority on forgiveness than on justice. We don't sing
"Amazing Justice"; we sing "Amazing
Grace." Justice didn't do a thing to heal me.
Forgiveness did.

Debbie Morris

*Bear with each other and forgive what-
ever grievances you may have against one
another. Forgive as the Lord forgave you.*

Colossians 3:13

*The name of our Lord Jesus . . . be glorified
in you, and you in him, according to the
grace of our God and the Lord Jesus Christ.*

2 Thessalonians 1:12

Love

❧

*T*he garment we find when we unwrap God's gift of grace is both the same for all his children and uniquely tailored to each one of us and our individual needs. We all receive grace to clothe ourselves so that we are prepared to walk with the King of Kings. Grace wraps us in the beauty of God's values and adorns our lives with the precious gems of his spiritual treasury.

Grace is not meant for only special occasions. I still tease my mom about her "good" clothes. When she buys a new suit or dress, it will hang in her wardrobe for eons, waiting for just the right occasion. I, on the other hand, most often try to squeeze into a new outfit in the car on my way home from the store. God's grace is not a suit meant for Sundays; we should wrap it around our shoulders every day of our lives.

Sheila Walsh

I delight greatly in the LORD; my soul rejoices in my God. For he has clothed me with garments of salvation and arrayed me in a robe of righteousness, as a bridegroom adorns his head like a priest, and as a bride adorns herself with her jewels.

❧Isaiah 61:10

We come into our relationship with God with all the flaws of a young bride but also with all the wonder, trust, and love. God, in turn, helps us to "grow up" in him.

Lord, thank you for love and the richness it provides. Thank you for creating within us the capacity to express that love. Thank you that you model for us the kind of love that rejoices over one another and that your love never dies. Amen.

Marilyn Meberg

For God so loved the world that he gave his one and only Son.

John 3:16

Follow the way of love.

1 Corinthians 14:1

A gift had been given that would never be taken from me. I knew this to be true because I had done absolutely nothing to earn it, and it was given me in my most unlovable hour. The joy that springs from grace is so different from mere happiness. I was happy when my brother graduated with distinction from university. I am happy when I listen to my sister sing. It always makes me happy to talk to my mom. Happy occasions have always helped me forget about the things that make me sad. But the experience of joy is different, deeper, because it knows the whole story. Grace embraced all that was good and true and all that was bad and faithless about me. Grace is love with its eyes wide open.

Sheila Walsh

Grace to all who love our Lord Jesus Christ with an undying love.

Ephesians 6:24

Because of his great love for us, God, who is rich in mercy, made us alive with Christ even when we were dead in transgressions—it is by grace you have been saved.

ℒEphesians 2:4–5

When winds are raging o'er the upper ocean,
And waves are tossed wild with an angry roar,
It's said, far down beneath the wild commotion,
That peaceful stillness reigns forevermore.
Far, far beneath, noise of tempests falls silent,
And silver waves lie ever peacefully,
And no storm, however fierce or violent,
Disturbs the Sabbath of that deeper sea.
So to the heart that knows Your love, O Father,
There is a temple sacred evermore,
And all life's angry voices causing bother
Die in hushed silence at its peaceful door.
Far, far away, the roars of strife fall silent,
And loving thoughts rise ever peacefully,
And no storm, however fierce or violent,
Disturbs the soul that dwells, O Lord, in Thee.

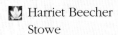 Harriet Beecher Stowe

Joy

❦

*J*oy can't be contained but must be free to come and go, which it will—just as trouble is never permanent. In the Lord, I am free of circumstance, whether good or bad. At the beginning of each day I make two choices: first, to accept trouble if it comes and to look for opportunities to do good in spite of how I feel. Second, never to cage joy if it alights on my shoulder.

Barbara Johnson

You will go out in joy and be led forth in peace; the mountains and hills will burst into song before you, and all the trees of the field will clap their hands.

Isaiah 55:12

*G*od, we might say, is in a good mood. He's not depressed. He's not misery seeking company. He's not some bitter, cosmic Neanderthal with his finger on a nuclear weapon. God is joy spilling over. This is where his mercy comes from.

The full tank of love God enjoys is splashing out over heaven's walls. He swims in elation and is driven to share it with us. Why? Simply, as he put it, "so that my joy may be in you" (John 15:11).

❧ Joni Eareckson Tada

*J*esus said, *"As the Father has loved me, so have I loved you. Now remain in my love.*
If you obey my commands, you will remain in my love, just as I have obeyed my Father's commands and remain in his love.
I have told you this so that my joy may be in you and that your joy may be complete."

❧John 15:9–11

As if she were looking right into my heart, Minnie Pearl told me, "You really won't know anything about laughing until you have found peace with God and love him first." There was something perfect about Miss Minnie's words—and their timing in my life. She had found me waiting backstage in the dark, longing to enjoy a good laugh. At that point in my life, very few professional colleagues knew anything about the layers of pain I was wearing around my heart. I can't see how Miss Minnie could have picked me out of those eight girls in the dressing room as the one carrying the greatest load of pain. I really thought I had disguised it so well. I wanted to know if my mother had called her and asked her to poke at my heart and remind me she was praying for my aching soul, trying to hurry the time along toward healing. How could she have known that what I was doing was standing, waiting, with my heart craning toward the slightest bit of light, longing to feel the morning sun across my face? How could she have known, in the darkest of my days, that what I was doing was waiting for the fun to come up? Miss Minnie's words set in motion a process that helped me find the fun, the fun that comes after the darkest night.

Chonda Pierce

The LORD *is my strength and my shield; my heart trusts in him, and I am helped. My heart leaps with joy and I will give thanks to him in song.*

⁖Psalm 28:7

"Instead of their shame my people will receive a double portion, and instead of disgrace they will rejoice in their inheritance; and so they will inherit a double portion in their land, and everlasting joy will be theirs. . . . In my faithfulness I will reward them and make an everlasting covenant with them. Their descendants will be known among the nations and their offspring among the peoples. All who see them will acknowledge that they are a people the LORD *has blessed."*

⁖Isaiah 61:7–9

115

When we receive God's grace, we can accept ourselves with all of our talents and our short-comings— and have true joy in who we are as a person.

There are different kinds of gifts, but the same Spirit. There are different kinds of service, but the same Lord. There are different kinds of working, but the same God works all of them . . . to each one the manifestation of the Spirit is given for the common good.

℘1 Corinthians 12:4–7

You have talent, skill, aptitude, and ability that are you-niquely yours. No two people sing, dance, paint, speak, organize, manage or teach just alike. When God made us, he made us special. We can be the best of what and who we want to be—and only God knows what our limitations are.

Thelma Wells

May he give you the desire of your heart and make all your plans succeed. We will shout for joy when you are victorious and will lift up our banners in the name of our God.

℘Psalm 20:4–5

Peace

❧

Build a little fence of trust
　　　Around today;
Fill the space with loving work
　　　And therein stay.
Look not through the protective rails
　　　Upon tomorrow;
God will help you bear what comes
　　　Of joy or sorrow.

Mary Butts

You will find it impossible to
"commit your way to the Lord" unless
your way has met with his approval. It
can only be done through faith, for if
there is even the slightest doubt in your
heart that your way is not a good one,
faith will refuse to have anything to do
with it. Also, this committing of your way
to him must be continuous, not just one
isolated action. And that is why some
Christians are so anxious and fearful.
They have obviously not truly committed
their way to the Lord and left it with him.
They took it to him but walked away with
it again.

L. B. Cowman

*D*o not be anxious about anything, but in everything, by prayer and petition, with thanksgiving, present your requests to God. And the peace of God, which transcends all understanding, will guard your hearts and your minds in Christ Jesus. . . . whatever is true, whatever is noble, whatever is right, whatever is pure, whatever is lovely, whatever is admirable —if anything is excellent or praiseworthy— think about such things. Whatever you have learned or received or heard from me, or seen in me—put it into practice. And the God of peace will be with you.

❧Philippians 4:6–9

*J*esus said, "Peace I leave with you; my peace I give you. I do not give to you as the world gives. Do not let your hearts be troubled and do not be afraid."

❧John 14:27

*U*nlike worldly peace, which is merely an absence of conflict, God can bring us peace even in the midst of our troubles.

❧NIV Spiritual Formation Bible

A king once offered a reward to the artist in his kingdom who best depicted the concept of peace on canvas. Myriad's of murals were submitted, but the one the king chose illustrated a mother bird building her nest into a rock behind a waterfall. While the bird wove her reeds into a nest, water cascaded powerfully before her. Unfazed by the roar about her, she knew she was in the right spot, and so she nested peacefully.

When I think of building a nest, my mind pictures secure sprigs nestled in a sturdy spruce. When the wind howls, I rush to add another twig. When the rains pelt, I flutter forth with more leaves to patch a leak. I view my role as mother to be one of guaranteeing safety and peace for my nest and all who dwell within. It's all up to me.

Could it be that safety and peace come not so much with my flitting and fluttering, but with where I choose to build my nest in the first place? Safe nests are those built in the Rock of a God who cares about every daily moment.

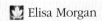 Elisa Morgan

Can you imagine how the world would be transformed if we all chose to live with gracious, generous hearts? Can you imagine the peace we would encounter if we set aside our petty differences and narrow-minded prejudices and embraced one another as we have been embraced by Christ? This kind of living would transform everything it came in contact with.

Sheila Walsh

What does the LORD require of you? To act justly and to love mercy and to walk humbly with your God.

Micah 6:8

LORD, you establish peace for us; all that we have accomplished you have done for us.

❧Isaiah 26:12

*Through the floodgates of God's mercy
Flowed a vast and gracious tide.
Grace and love like mighty rivers
Poured incessant from above;
And heaven's peace and perfect justice
Kissed a guilty world in love.*

❧Traditional

A great company of the heavenly host appeared with the angel, praising God and saying, "Glory to God in the highest, and on earth peace to men on whom his favor rests."

❧Luke 2:13–14

Since we have been justified through faith, we have peace with God through our Lord Jesus Christ, through whom we have gained access by faith into this grace in which we now stand. And we rejoice in the hope of the glory of God.

❧Romans 5:1–2

I will lift my voice and sing
'Cause your love does amazing things
Lord, I know
My life is in your hands

So I will find my rest
And I will find my peace
Knowing that
You'll meet my every need.

When I'm at my weakest
Oh, you carry me
Then I become my strongest
Lord, in your hands.

There is no situation in this life that God will
not miraculously lead us through—giving us a
strength and peace that we know is beyond
anything we could conjure up. Lean on him.
Abandon yourself to his grace. God will give
you strength when you need it.

Kathy Troccoli

*There is a time for everything, and a
season for every activity under heaven:
a time to be born and a time to die, a time
to plant and a time to uproot,
a time to kill and a time to heal, a time to
tear down and a time to build,
a time to weep and a time to laugh, a time
to mourn and a time to dance,
a time to scatter stones and a time to gather
them, a time to embrace and a time to
refrain,
a time to search and a time to give up, a
time to keep and a time to throw away,
a time to tear and a time to mend, a time
to be silent and a time to speak,
a time to love and a time to hate, a time for
war and a time for peace.*

&Ecclesiastes 3:1–8

Patience

๕

*W*hen we allow the Holy Spirit to adorn
our hearts with patience, we find his wisdom
in daily living—practical things that we never
imagined could take on a spiritual meaning.
These all become a part of our personal style
in our walk with God that both lifts us up to
see his perspective on the great matters of the
universe and causes us to fall to our knees and
humbly regard the tiniest flower as his master-
piece of creation.

*A*nd we pray this in order that you may live
a life worthy of the Lord and may please him in
every way: bearing fruit in every good work,
growing in the knowledge of God, being
strengthened with all power according to his
glorious might so that you may have great
endurance and patience, and joyfully giving
thanks to the Father, who has qualified you to
share in the inheritance of the saints in the
kingdom of light.

๕Colossians 1:10–12

What does it mean to "wait for the Lord"? Well, some people think of the kind of waiting you do because you're forced to. (Like when there are ten people ahead of you at the doctor's office, and you kill time flipping through magazines.) But when the Bible talks about waiting, it means confidently trusting that God knows how much suffering I need and can take. It means looking expectantly toward the time when he will free me from my burdens.

❧ Joni Eareckson Tada

He has made everything beautiful in its time. He has also set eternity in the hearts of men; yet they cannot fathom what God has done from beginning to end. I know that there is nothing better for men than to be happy and do good while they live.

Ecclesiastes 3:11–12

$\mathcal{P}$atience is not the same thing as resignation or the cynical attitude that always expects the worst possible outcome. Patience is a more positive trait. It is the ability to bear affliction, delay and interruption with calmness, perseverance and confidence in the goodness of God. It is inward peace as well as outward control. It is the submission of our schedules, our viewpoints, our dreams to the greater plan of God, with the conviction that he has a good reason for every delay he allows to come our way.

Barbara Bush

$\mathcal{I}$mitate those who through faith and patience inherit what has been promised.

Hebrews 6:12

Now the LORD was gracious to Sarah as he had said, and the LORD did for Sarah what he had promised. Sarah became pregnant and bore a son to Abraham in his old age, at the very time God had promised him. Abraham gave the name Isaac to the son Sarah bore him. When his son Isaac was eight days old, Abraham circumcised him, as God commanded him. Abraham was a hundred years old when his son Isaac was born to him. Sarah said, "God has brought me laughter, and everyone who hears about this will laugh with me." And she added, "Who would have said to Abraham that Sarah would nurse children? Yet I have borne him a son in his old age."

❧Genesis 21:1–7

Therefore, as God's chosen people, holy and dearly loved, clothe yourselves with compassion, kindness, humility, gentleness and patience.

❧Colossians 3:12

As an example of patience in the face of suffering, take the prophets who spoke in the name of the Lord. As you know, we consider blessed those who have persevered. You have heard of Job's perseverance and have seen what the Lord finally brought about. The Lord is full of compassion and mercy.

❧James 5:10–11

Kindness

৵

One time when I was feeling low, I received a call from a friend whose husband was in intensive care. I didn't want to go out in the cold and the dark to be with her that night at the hospital. She didn't say, "I need you." She told me, "You don't have to come." I went anyway.

The hospital seemed so impersonal. White walls led down corridors of unmarked doors. Out-of-date magazines were sprawled across tables in the waiting area. I found my friend looking small and alone. When she saw me, tears flowed down her cheeks. I found myself starting to cry with my friend. Pretty soon we were hugging one another in that hospital room where a good man was dying.

The years have come and gone since that night, but still ringing in my heart is the Scripture, "Weep with them that weep" (Romans 12:15 KJV). Sometimes the right words are no words at all. Sometimes the best strength is no strength at all.

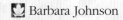 Barbara Johnson

The fruit of the Spirit is love, joy, peace, patience, kindness, goodness, faithfulness, gentleness and self-control.

⁓Galatians 5:22–23

Carry each other's burdens, and in this way you will fulfill the law of Christ.

⁓Galatians 6:2

Since we live by the Spirit, let us keep in step with the Spirit.

⁓Galatians 5:25

Keep yourselves in God's love as you wait for the mercy of our Lord Jesus Christ to bring you to eternal life.

⁓Jude 21

Two are better than one, because they have a good return for their work: If one falls down, his friend can help him up. But pity the man who falls and has no one to help him up! Also, if two lie down together, they will keep warm. But how can one keep warm alone? Though one may be overpowered, two can defend themselves. A cord of three strands is not quickly broken.

⁓Ecclesiastes 4:9–12

God himself set the example of how to love by living and dying in service to the unlovely. His humble birth into human form— all for the love of humankind—was outrageous! God's very ordinariness is a stunning insult to the proud, a tender delight to the grateful. Every day we are also called to live extraordinary lives in ordinary ways.

Thelma Wells

God raised us up with Christ and seated us with him in the heavenly realms in Christ Jesus, in order that in the coming ages he might show the incomparable riches of his grace, expressed in his kindness to us in Christ Jesus. For it is by grace you have been saved, through faith—and this not from yourselves, it is the gift of God— not by works, so that no one can boast. For we are God's workmanship, created in Christ Jesus to do good works, which God prepared in advance for us to do.

Ephesians 2:6–10

Now Elimelech, Naomi's husband, died, and she was left with her two sons. They married Moabite women, one named Orpah and the other Ruth. After they had lived there about ten years, both Mahlon and Kilion also died, and Naomi was left without her two sons and her husband.

. . .Then Naomi said to her two daughters-in-law, "Go back, each of you, to your mother's home. May the LORD show kindness to you, as you have shown to your dead and to me. May the LORD grant that each of you will find rest in the home of another husband."

. . . But Ruth replied, "Don't urge me to leave you or to turn back from you. Where you go I will go, and where you stay I will stay. Your people will be my people and your God my God. Where you die I will die, and there I will be buried. May the LORD deal with me, be it ever so severely, if anything but death separates you and me."

❧Ruth 1:3–5, 8, 16

Consider the woman who broke her jar of expensive perfume over the feet of Jesus. Even though she was criticized by others for the recklessness of her act, Christ reprimanded her critics, telling them they did not understand what she had done. There is no better moment to pour your love out on another. Carpe diem: Seize the day!

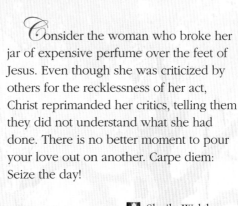 Sheila Walsh

Dear friends, let us love one another, for love comes from God. Everyone who loves has been born of God and knows God.

❧1 John 4:7

Now one of the Pharisees invited Jesus to
have dinner with him, so he went to the
Pharisee's house and reclined at the table.
When a woman who had lived a sinful life in
that town learned that Jesus was eating at the
Pharisee's house, she brought an alabaster jar
of perfume, and as she stood behind him at his
feet weeping, she began to wet his feet with her
tears. Then she wiped them with her hair,
kissed them and poured perfume on them.
Then he turned toward the woman and said to
Simon, "Do you see this woman? I came into
your house. You did not give me any water for
my feet, but she wet my feet with her tears and
wiped them with her hair. You did not give me
a kiss, but this woman, from the time I entered,
has not stopped kissing my feet. You did not put
oil on my head, but she has poured perfume on
my feet. Therefore, I tell you, her many sins
have been forgiven —for she loved much. But
he who has been forgiven little loves little."

❧Luke 7:36–38, 44–47

Goodness

❧

*W*hy are so many of us hung up on our spiritual performance? And I say "us" because I know I've got a lot of company out there in "Believer Land." We feel guilty that we haven't prayed enough, memorized or studied Scripture enough, witnessed enough, fasted and prayed enough, supported or adopted enough orphans, served on enough church committees, or baked enough cookies for shut-ins, and so on. These are the kinds of thoughts and emotions that cause us to turn from the Light. The next thing we know we're back in that dark place groping about for a candle. But to be free means we don't have to be anything or do anything. We can stop constantly evaluating ourselves.

I used to worry that if I took grace that literally, I'd quit working to further the kingdom of God. I feared that a relaxed acceptance of God's grace would encourage a slothful, lazy, maybe even indifferent approach to living that would land me in a hammock somewhere tossing berries in the air and counting the number that actually fell into my mouth. However, that has not been the case at all. Instead I have found that grace so softens and moves my spirit, touches so deeply that core of gratitude within me, that I want to serve him.

🌷 Marilyn Meberg

*W*hat enriches your spirit? Filling your heart and mind with whatever is true, noble, right, pure, lovely, admirable, or anything excellent or praiseworthy.

What enriches your spirit? Accessing the means of grace through prayer, worship, the reading of God's Word, and fellowship.

Joni Eareckson Tada

*J*esus said, *"Remain in me, and I will remain in you. No branch can bear fruit by itself; it must remain in the vine. Neither can you bear fruit unless you remain in me."*

John 15:4

*C*harm is deceptive, and beauty is fleeting; but a woman who fears the LORD is to be praised.

Proverbs 31:30

*A*ll we have to do is humble ourselves before God. As we move toward him, we will see him running to meet us.

🌸 Sheila Walsh

We have different gifts, according to the grace given us. If a man's gift is prophesying, let him use it in proportion to his faith. If it is serving, let him serve; if it is teaching, let him teach; if it is encouraging, let him encourage; if it is contributing to the needs of others, let him give generously; if it is leadership, let him govern diligently; if it is showing mercy, let him do it cheerfully. Love must be sincere. Hate what is evil; cling to what is good.

❧Romans 12:6–9

God made him who had no sin to be sin for us, so that in him we might become the righteousness of God. As God's fellow workers we urge you not to receive God's grace in vain. For he says, "In the time of my favor I heard you, and in the day of salvation I helped you." I tell you, now is the time of God's favor, now is the day of salvation.

❧2 Corinthians 5:21

Faithfulness

❧

The lessons of friendship were deeply ingrained in me growing up—discipline; patience; self-sacrifice; how to create fun out of frustration, persist with others through all kinds of trials, and ride over the storm, knowing that behind the clouds, the sun was always shining; accepting what is; enjoying the good times; persevering through the bad.

🍁 Joy MacKenzie

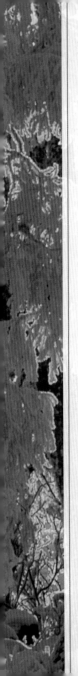

So then, just as you received Christ Jesus as Lord, continue to live in him, rooted and built up in him, strengthened in the faith as you were taught, and overflowing with thankfulness. See to it that no one takes you captive through hollow and deceptive philosophy, which depends on human tradition and the basic principles of this world rather than on Christ.

Colossians 2:6–8

O LORD, our Lord, how majestic is your name in all the earth! You have set your glory above the heavens.
From the lips of children and infants you have ordained praise.
When I consider your heavens, the work of your fingers, the moon and the stars, which you have set in place,
what is man that you are mindful of him, the son of man that you care for him?
You made him a little lower than the heavenly beings and crowned him with glory and honor.
O LORD, our Lord, how majestic is your name in all the earth!

Psalm 8:1–5, 9

*A*lthough Catherine Booth, co-founder of the Salvation Army, was, in her own words, "one of the most timid and bashful disciples the Lord Jesus ever saved," she was well-prepared for her public ministry. She had been active in the temperance movement and was well versed in Scripture. She had been a Bible student from the time she was a child. By the time she was twelve she had read the Bible through eight times. By nineteenth-century standards, she enjoyed freedom accorded few married women, and her husband William apparently was not threatened by the potential competition of her ministry. Soon after her pulpit debut, William became ill, and his slow recovery opened the door for her own preaching ministry. For a time he was so ill that she took over his entire circuit. She was a dynamic and forceful speaker. Catherine's only regret was that she had waited so long to begin.

Catherine was involved in city mission work, and it was through this common interest with her husband that the Salvation Army was born.

 Ruth Tucker

*J*ohn Wesley wrote a memorial titled "That Burning and Shining Light" for Jane Cooper, a faithful leader in the early Methodist church in England:

In the latter end of this year, God called to himself that burning and shining light, Jane Cooper. As she was both a living and a dying witness of Christian perfection, it will not be at all foreign to the subject to add a short account of her death; with one of her own letters, containing a plain and artless relation of the manner wherein it pleased God to work that great change in her soul:

"The Lord, the King, was in the midst of me, and that I should see evil no more. I now blessed him who had visited and redeemed me, and was become my 'wisdom, righteousness, sanctification, and redemption.' I saw Jesus altogether lovely; and knew he was mine in all his offices. And, glory be to him, he now reigns in my heart without a rival. I find no will but his. I feel no pride; nor any affection but what is placed on him. I know it is by faith I stand; and that watching unto prayer must be the guard of faith. I am happy in God this moment, and I believe for the next. . . . I desire to be lost in that 'love which passeth knowledge.' I see 'the just shall live by faith'; and unto me, who am less than the least of all saints, is this grace given."

 Jane Cooper

*T*hroughout the centuries, the "call" was a very important factor in justifying a woman's roll in Christian ministry. Women often testified of their reservations about entering a man's domain, but that they finally relented and obeyed the voice of God. Jarena Lee, the first widely traveled woman preacher of the African Methodist Episcopal Church, testified to such an experience:

"Between four and five years after my sanctification, on a certain time, an impressive silence fell upon me, and I stood as if someone was about to speak to me, yet I had no such thought in my heart. But to my utter surprise there seemed to sound a voice which I thought I distinctly heard, and most certainly understood, which said to me 'Go preach the Gospel!' I immediately replied aloud, 'No one will believe me.' Again I listened, and again the same voice seemed to say, 'Preach the Gospel; I will put words in your mouth.'"

 Ruth Tucker

*J*arena Lee, a faithful woman evangelist during the 1800's, wrote this about her first encounter with God as a member of the African Methodist Episcopal Church:

That moment, though hundreds were present, I did leap to my feet, and declare that God, for Christ's sake, had pardoned the sins of my soul. Great was the ecstasy of my mind, for I felt that not only the sin of malice was pardoned, but all other sins were swept away together. That day was the first when my heart had believed, and my tongue had made confession unto salvation—the first words uttered, a part of that song which shall fill eternity with its sound, were "Glory to God." For a few moments I had power to exhort sinners, and to tell of the wonders and of the goodness of him who had clothed me with his salvation. During this, the minister was silent, until my soul felt its duty had been performed. Then he declared another witness of the power of Christ to forgive sins on earth was manifest in my conversion.

Jarena Lee, 1836

Gentleness

❧

*J*esus longs to hold you, to care for you. He longs to meet your needs and for you to put your trust in him. He is a faithful God with arms that will never let you go. Ask me why I love him and you'll receive the same response that I received from a little boy named Jordan. He's my friend. He's my hero. He's my everything.

🌷 Kathy Troccoli

*L*et your gentleness be evident to all. The Lord is near.

❧Philippians 4:5

*T*herefore, as God's chosen people, holy and dearly loved, clothe yourselves with compassion, kindness, humility, gentleness and patience.

❧Colossians 3:12

*P*ursue righteousness, godliness, faith, love, endurance and gentleness.

❧1 Timothy 6:11

By the meekness and gentleness of Christ, I appeal to you —I, Paul, who am "timid" when face to face with you, but "bold" when away! I beg you that when I come I may not have to be as bold as I expect to be toward some people who think that we live by the standards of this world. For though we live in the world, we do not wage war as the world does. The weapons we fight with are not the weapons of the world. On the contrary, they have divine power to demolish strongholds. We demolish arguments and every pretension that sets itself up against the knowledge of God, and we take captive every thought to make it obedient to Christ.

❧2 Corinthians 10:1–5

Love of my soul,
You are my light in the darkness;
You are the breath in my body.
Your love fills me up
As food does the hungry.

When I am weary,
You carry me in your arms.
When I fall,
You pick me up again.

You are my strength;
You are my joy.
You are the one who has
Taught me how to love.

With you in my life,
I feel safe.
It feels as if no harm
Could come to me.

You give me the courage
To go on when I think that
All is lost.

Your love lifts me up
To the highest place,
And my happiness
Exceeds all else.

I love you
With all that
Is in me,
With all I have.

Without you, I
Would be lost.
I don't know
Where I'd go.

You've made my
Life complete,
And with your love,
I can be whole.

I love you more
with every passing day.
My joy continues to grow
Into a sea of dreams.

You can make those
Dreams come true
With your love.
My love is for you.

Iris Schrimpf

Discipline

❧

God doesn't stop loving us even when we do the wrong thing. God's love is not like cotton candy—sweet, cheap, and easy to digest. It cost him everything, and its demands on us can be hard to swallow. In response to his love, we are called to love as well: love him, love our neighbors, love our enemies.

God never just leaves his people to dwell in their sinful unworthiness indefinitely. Even his discipline for misbehavior is always within the nurturing, protective environment of his love.

The entire book of Hosea gives us a metaphorical picture of God (Hosea) loving his people (Gomer) in spite of their unfaithfulness. The Israelites were an unruly, sin-loving, idol-worshiping, multitudinous gang of rebels who sometimes during the passing of centuries loved and obeyed God, but more often than not said, "What the hey. . . let's party!" Though grieved and often angry, God stuck by them. Why? Because he'd promised to never leave them, and God doesn't break his promises, even when we do!

Marilyn Meberg

One of the main reasons we need to pray with an "if-it-be-Thy-will" attitude is that it's so easy for us to make mistakes and misread God's will. Countless times I have fooled myself into believing the prayers I prayed were for God's glory when actually they were for myself.

Joni Eareckson Tada

You are my portion, O LORD; I have promised to obey your words. I have sought your face with all my heart; be gracious to me according to your promise. I have considered my ways and have turned my steps to your statutes. I will hasten and not delay to obey your commands.

Psalm 119:57–60

Endure hardship with us like a good soldier of Christ Jesus. No one serving as a soldier gets involved in civilian affairs—he wants to please his commanding officer. Similarly, if anyone competes as an athlete, he does not receive the victor's crown unless he competes according to the rules. The hardworking farmer should be the first to receive a share of the crops. Reflect on what I am saying, for the Lord will give you insight into all this.

2 Timothy 2:3–7

*You who fear the LORD, praise him!
All you descendants of Jacob, honor him!
Revere him, all you descendants of Israel!
For he has not despised or disdained
the suffering of the afflicted one;
he has not hidden his face from him
The poor will eat and be satisfied;
they who seek the LORD will praise him—
may your hearts live forever!
All the ends of the earth
will remember and turn to the LORD,
and all the families of the nations
will bow down before him.*

❧Psalm 22:23, 24, 26, 27

*As a father has compassion on his children,
so the LORD has compassion on those who fear him;
for he knows how we are formed,
he remembers that we are dust.*

❧Psalm 103: 13–14

God's
Grace
extended
Through Us

To Our Family

❧

*W*hen we receive the gift of grace from our Lord, our lives are changed from within so that his beauty is what radiates from us as we walk this earth. And that can change the world one heart at a time starting with our families. On our own we feel inadequate to the challenge, but trusting in God's grace we know we can make a difference as women of faith.

*W*e will tell the next generation the praiseworthy deeds of the LORD, his power, and the wonders he has done.

❧Psalm 78:4

*T*hese commandments that I give you today are to be upon your hearts. Impress them on your children. Talk about them when you sit at home and when you walk along the road, when you lie down and when you get up. Tie them as symbols on your hands and bind them on your foreheads. Write them on the doorframes of your houses and on your gates.

❧Deuteronomy 6:6–9

*W*e worship not only on our knees but also as we live our lives. Our everyday lives are important to God, important enough that he sent his Son to die on the cross so that Jesus could live in us through each day—including the ordinary ones.

We can now say: "I'm going to school to worship God," "I'm going to paint a picture to worship God," "I'm going to clean the kitchen to worship God," "I'm going to my job to worship God," as well as "I'm going to church to worship God."

It is a challenge to live our lives as sacrifices to God. All that we do or think must conform to the Word of God. Such a high calling is impossible without the Holy Spirit's guidance and help.

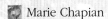 Marie Chapian

My mother died of cancer. She showed amazing courage throughout her illness and handled the dying process with dignity and humility. She was prodded, poked, operated on, and carted back and forth to hospitals, but she never once complained, only confessed that she was "getting tired." Before my eyes she lived out the truth of another of her favorite phrases: "God will give you strength when you need it."

Of all the words my mother spoke, I think that statement has meant the most. When I was in the middle of the most difficult times of my life—the struggles, the tears, the dark days—she would offer those tender words. Now, as I look back and see that God really was with me, giving me grace to bear the unbearable, I realize that my mother was right.

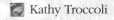 Kathy Troccoli

God sets the lonely in families.

✞Psalm 68:6

Jesus said, "Go home to your family and tell them how much the Lord has done for you, and how he has had mercy on you."

✞Mark 5:19

Let us not become weary in doing good, for at the proper time we will reap a harvest if we do not give up. Therefore, as we have opportunity, let us do good to all people, especially to those who belong to the family of believers.

✞Galatians 6:9–10

Grace and peace be yours in abundance through the knowledge of God and of Jesus our Lord. His divine power has given us everything we need for life and godliness through our knowledge of him who called us by his own glory and goodness. Through these he has given us his very great and precious promises, so that through them you may participate in the divine nature and escape the corruption in the world caused by evil desires. For this very reason, make every effort to add to your faith goodness; and to goodness, knowledge; and to knowledge, self-control; and to self-control, perseverance; and to perseverance, godliness; and to godliness, brotherly kindness; and to brotherly kindness, love.

✞2 Peter 1:2-7

*S*ometimes it is our example that portrays God's grace to our families and other times we are the one who learn a lesson about our heavenly father from the example of faithful members of our family—when we have our spiritual eyes and ears open we may receive a blessing by seeing a reflection of grace in those closest to us!

Many Sundays, it would have been easier for Dad to stay at home, but like the gardener who pays attention to his plot of earth, Dad was faithful! His life was so woven into the fabric of this close-knit family of God's people, I wondered if they could possibly know how much they meant to him. Many Sundays he played the organ when his load was heavy and his heart was broken. Isn't that like the heavenly Father? So generously faithful, he pays attention to our needs. He loves us so much he sends us the rain and sun and, in due time, harvest.

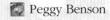 Peggy Benson

$\mathcal{B}$e shepherds of God's flock that is under your care, serving as overseers— not because you must, but because you are willing, as God wants you to be . . . not lording it over those entrusted to you, but being examples to the flock.

❧1 Peter 5:2–3

"$\mathcal{B}$lessed are the poor in spirit, for theirs is the kingdom of heaven.
Blessed are those who mourn, for they will be comforted.
Blessed are the meek, for they will inherit the earth.
Blessed are those who hunger and thirst for righteousness, for they will be filled.
Blessed are the merciful, for they will be shown mercy.
Blessed are the pure in heart, for they will see God.
Blessed are the peacemakers, for they will be called sons of God."

❧Matthew 5:2–12

*I*n my heart I know the rarest thing we'll ever grow is the deep friendship that will never die with any season. Someone has said, "You can't take it with you," but I am convinced that what my sister and I have grown together is already being transplanted in the perfected Garden of Eden on the sunny banks of Jordan.

Our mother's illness and ultimate death from cancer was a bittersweet process we shared together. It made me love Evelyn all the more to share the experience no one can put into words. We hold to each other more tightly than ever, treasuring every stolen moment together—each opportunity to share insights from what life is teaching us, each exchange of cute or brilliant antics of our grandchildren. We trade plants from our gardens in the spring and give each other seeds in the fall. We take trips to the nurseries to buy new breeds of geraniums or find unusual perennials.

Gloria Gaither

If a widow has children or grandchildren, these should learn first of all to put their religion into practice by caring for their own family and so repaying their parents and grandparents, for this is pleasing to God.
If anyone does not provide for his relatives, and especially for his immediate family, he has denied the faith and is worse than an unbeliever.

᠃1 Timothy 5:4,8

Be kind and compassionate to one another, forgiving each other, just as in Christ God forgave you. Be imitators of God, therefore, as dearly loved children and live a life of love, just as Christ loved us and gave himself up for us as a fragrant offering and sacrifice to God.

᠃Ephesians 4:32—5:2

Now that you have purified yourselves by obeying the truth so that you have sincere love for your brothers, love one another deeply, from the heart.

᠃1 Peter 1:22

159

I can always tell if the birds are working on their nest outside my kitchen window by their songs in the early morning. Long before I can see them, I can hear their music. Sure enough, when I gently raise the blinds and sneak a peek outside, there is Mom tucked into her birdhouse hole and Dad watching guard on a branch of a nearby tree. While she sits and he flies and brings food, they sing.

They are committed to each other, to their nest, and to the hopes of their brood. Not a bad lot in life, really. And I look back over my life with a greater appreciation.

While your days may be filled with too many Legos under your feet and not enough time alone, what do you have to sing about? If you had to come up with twenty items under the heading, "Thank you, God, for" could you? Put aside the things you would "die to have" and jot down a mental list of what you do have.

You don't have to be an accomplished musician to hum a song of praise. Move it through your mind in the shower. Hum it quietly at the sink. Put words to it and belt it out in the car. Give yourself something to sing about in your mind and with your voice, and when you've finished the second verse, you'll probably have a song in your heart.

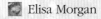 Elisa Morgan

If we are children of God and joint heirs with Jesus, we have the attributes of our spiritual relatives—enough love, understanding, forgiveness, power, and grace.

You can do it. You can treat your enemies with love and respect even as they mistreat you. You can love your neighbors as you love yourself, even if they throw trash in your yard and yell at your children. You can forgive the ugly things people have done and said to you, and pardon them as God has pardoned you. No, it's not easy. But the practice of perfect makes perfect. Start practicing today by asking God to remove all the blocks that have kept you from forgiving and loving people. Talk to a Christian friend who will listen to your hurts and give you Scripture-based advice on how to respond. Most important, follow the example of Jesus, "the author and perfecter of our faith, who for the joy set before him endured the cross, scorning its shame, and sat down at the right hand of the throne of God."

 Thelma Wells

Let the word of Christ dwell in you richly as you teach and admonish one another with all wisdom, and as you sing psalms, hymns and spiritual songs with gratitude in your hearts to God.

❧Colossians 3:16

"When you enter a house, first say, 'Peace to this house.' If a man of peace is there, your peace will rest on him; if not, it will return to you."

❧Luke 10:5–6

I would like our home to be a place where friendships can grow, blossom, and mature— where deep friendships thrive alongside fragile new ones. I would teach our children that the greatest Friend of all is the God of the Universe, who cared so much that he chose to walk the dusty roads of earth with us. God confined his great mind to our finite thoughts and expressed his unfathomable truths in the words of a human language. He exchanged the grandeur of heaven for a simple carpenter's home, a friend's guest room, and a borrowed tomb. And he traded having us all as his slaves and servants for enjoying us as his friends.

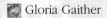 Gloria Gaither

To Our Church

❦

If I speak in the tongues of men and of angels, but have not love, I am only a resounding gong or a clanging cymbal.

If I have the gift of prophecy and can fathom all mysteries and all knowledge, and if I have a faith that can move mountains, but have not love, I am nothing.

If I give all I possess to the poor and surrender my body to the flames, but have not love, I gain nothing.

Love is patient, love is kind. It does not envy, it does not boast, it is not proud.

It is not rude, it is not self-seeking, it is not easily angered, it keeps no record of wrongs.

Love does not delight in evil but rejoices with the truth.

It always protects, always trusts, always hopes, always perseveres.

Love never fails.

And now these three remain: faith, hope and love. But the greatest of these is love.

❦1 Corinthians 13:1–8,13

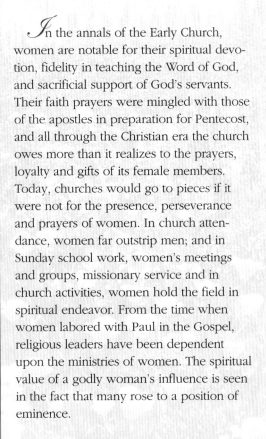

*I*n the annals of the Early Church, women are notable for their spiritual devotion, fidelity in teaching the Word of God, and sacrificial support of God's servants. Their faith prayers were mingled with those of the apostles in preparation for Pentecost, and all through the Christian era the church owes more than it realizes to the prayers, loyalty and gifts of its female members. Today, churches would go to pieces if it were not for the presence, perseverance and prayers of women. In church attendance, women far outstrip men; and in Sunday school work, women's meetings and groups, missionary service and in church activities, women hold the field in spiritual endeavor. From the time when women labored with Paul in the Gospel, religious leaders have been dependent upon the ministries of women. The spiritual value of a godly woman's influence is seen in the fact that many rose to a position of eminence.

Women were the last to leave the cross, first at the tomb on Christ's resurrection day, and the first to proclaim the glorious news of his victory o'er the grave.

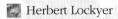 Herbert Lockyer

Yes, and I ask you, loyal yokefellow, help these women who have contended at my side in the cause of the gospel, along with Clement and the rest of my fellow workers, whose names are in the book of life.

❧Philippians 4:3

Leaving the next day, we reached Caesarea and stayed at the house of Philip the evangelist, one of the Seven. He had four unmarried daughters who prophesied.

❧Acts 21:8-9

I commend to you our sister Phoebe, a servant of the church in Cenchrea. I ask you to receive her in the Lord in a way worthy of the saints and to give her any help she may need from you, for she has been a great help to many people, including me. Greet Priscilla and Aquila, my fellow workers in Christ Jesus. They risked their lives for me. Not only I but all the churches of the Gentiles are grateful to them.

❧Romans 16:1–4

*L*ooking back on my life, I can see countless times when God sent messengers of hope and comfort to me. A neighbor who fixed an extra casserole for our supper or vacuumed the living room before unexpected guests arrived. A funny story that brought a reprieve from a busy day. A prosthetic bra saleswoman! An assuring Post-it note. A simple message on the little square of yellow brought such peace to me—somewhere out there someone was awake and praying for my brand-new son. (If you possess Post-it notes, you have the potential to be a great encourager—don't squander your opportunities.)

The timing of the message—as always when God is involved—was incredible and perfect. And it will be tomorrow too. The question is, are we listening for him?

 Chonda Pierce

We are God's workmanship, created in Christ Jesus to do good works, which God prepared in advance for us to do.

❧Ephesians 2:10

God is able to make all grace abound to you, so that in all things at all times, having all that you need, you will abound in every good work.

❧2 Corinthians 9:8

To each one of us grace has been given as Christ apportioned it. This is why it says: "When he ascended on high, he led captives in his train and gave gifts to men."

❧Ephesians 4:7–8

Do not withhold good from those who deserve it, when it is in your power to act. Do not say to your neighbor, "Come back later; I'll give it tomorrow"— when you now have it with you.

❧Proverbs 3:21–28

*A*manda Smith was born a slave in Maryland and grew up experiencing hard work and intense religious emotion. "Red hot" camp meeting revivalism often provided her only leisure-time activity. She was married twice. Her first husband abandoned her, and her second husband died. After that she heard a distinct call from God to preach. She spent years traveling throughout America in the post-Civil War South and North, as well as England, India, and Africa, where she evangelized and preached to all races.

In her writing, Amanda Smith told how her ministry was deeply influenced by the modeling of her mother and grandmother, who, not unlike countless other slave women in the antebellum South, overcame the drudgery of their day-to-day toil by sharing their faith and religious experience with others—often their mistresses and their families. So strong was the influence of these slave women that one young mistress wanted to go to the "colored people's church." Her family "would not have that. So they kept her from going . . . About a quarter of a mile away was the great dairy, and Miss Celie used to slip over there when she got a chance and have a good time praying with mother and grandmother."

 Ruth Tucker

You have taken off your old self with its practices and have put on the new self, which is being renewed in knowledge in the image of its Creator.

Here there is no Greek or Jew, circumcised or uncircumcised, barbarian, Scythian, slave or free, but Christ is all, and is in all. Therefore, as God's chosen people, holy and dearly loved, clothe yourselves with compassion, kindness, humility, gentleness and patience.

Bear with each other and forgive whatever grievances you may have against one another. Forgive as the Lord forgave you. And over all these virtues put on love, which binds them all together in perfect unity.

Let the peace of Christ rule in your hearts, since as members of one body you were called to peace. And be thankful.

Let the word of Christ dwell in you richly as you teach and admonish one another with all wisdom, and as you sing psalms, hymns and spiritual songs with gratitude in your hearts to God.

And whatever you do, whether in word or deed, do it all in the name of the Lord Jesus, giving thanks to God the Father through him.

❧Colossians 3:9–17

We continually remember before our God and Father your work produced by faith, your labor prompted by love, and your endurance inspired by hope in our Lord Jesus Christ.

❧1 Thessalonians 1:3

If we walk in the light, as he is in the light, we have fellowship with one another, and the blood of Jesus, his Son, purifies us from all sin.

❧1 John 1:7

It was not through law that Abraham and his offspring received the promise that he would be heir of the world, but through the righteousness that comes by faith. . . . The promise comes by faith, so that it may be by grace and may be guaranteed to all Abraham's offspring—not only to those who are of the law but also to those who are of the faith of Abraham. He is the father of us all. As it is written: "I have made you a father of many nations." He is our father in the sight of God.

❧Romans 4:13–17

Teach me your way, O Lord, and I will walk in your truth; give me an undivided heart, that I may fear your name. I will praise you, O Lord my God, with all my heart; I will glorify your name forever.

❧Psalm 86:11-12

Since you are eager to have spiritual gifts, try to excel in gifts that build up the church.

❧1 Corinthians 14:12

I urge you to live a life worthy of the calling you have received. Be completely humble and gentle; be patient, bearing with one another in love. Make every effort to keep the unity of the Spirit through the bond of peace. There is one body and one Spirit—just as you were called to one hope when you were called—one Lord, one faith, one baptism; one God and Father of all, who is over all and through all and in all.

❧Ephesians 4:1–6

Set an example for the believers in speech, in life, in love, in faith and in purity. Until I come, devote yourself to the public reading of Scripture, to preaching and to teaching. Do not neglect your gift, which was given you through a prophetic message when the body of elders laid their hands on you. Be diligent in these matters; give yourself wholly to them, so that everyone may see your progress. Watch your life and doctrine closely. Persevere in them, because if you do, you will save both yourself and your hearers.

❧1 Timothy 4:12–16

The longer I live the more convinced I become that real wisdom and real intelligence and true greatness belong to us only when we get big enough to become as a little child and believe in a Jesus who can make a difference in the way we live. We are rich because, as the highest of God's creation, he gave us the ability to love back, to return the affection. It is almost as great to be able to love back as it is to know you are loved. I don't believe in having a religion, but this thing of serving Jesus, betting everything you are and have on a way that is beyond proof, really works.

Gloria Gaither

Jesus said, "Do not look down on one of these little ones. For I tell you that their angels in heaven always see the face of my Father."

Matthew 18:10

We have different gifts, according to the grace given us.

ॐRomans 12:6

Oh, that I could forever sit,
Like Mary, at the Master's feet:
     Be this my happy choice:
My only care, delight and bliss,
My joy, my Heaven on earth be this,
     To hear the Bridegroom's voice.

Charles Wesley

As Jesus and his disciples were on their way, he came to a village where a woman named Martha opened her home to him. She had a sister called Mary, who sat at the Lord's feet listening to what he said. But Martha was distracted by all the preparations that had to be made. She came to him and asked, "Lord, don't you care that my sister has left me to do the work by myself? Tell her to help me!"

"Martha, Martha," the Lord answered, "you are worried and upset about many things, but only one thing is needed. Mary has chosen what is better, and it will not be taken away from her."

ॐLuke 10:3—42

I always thank God for you because of his grace given you in Christ Jesus. For in him you have been enriched in every way—in all your speaking and in all your knowledge.

❧1 Corinthians 1:4

Because of his great love for us, God, who is rich in mercy, made us alive with Christ even when we were dead in transgressions—it is by grace you have been saved.

❧Ephesians 2:4–5

Be kind and compassionate to one another, forgiving each other, just as in Christ God forgave you.

❧Ephesians 4:32

There are different kinds of gifts, but the same Spirit. There are different kinds of service, but the same Lord. There are different kinds of working, but the same God works all of them in all men. Now to each one the manifestation of the Spirit is given for the common good.

❧1 Corinthians 12:4–7

*A*s women of faith we have been empowered by the gospel to share God's grace just like the first disciples of Jesus who went out without seminary degrees (and even without a purse!) to spread the good news in their own towns and homes. Instead of sending those who need help to a church, we bring the church to them. Instead of sending the seeker to a counselor or sage, we bring the Holy Spirit, our own loving Counselor, along with us. It is though God's grace we come to accept ourselves and extend that acceptance that can transform lives.

Pat Matuszak

*T*rue transformation is not something you work at with your own strength any more than a caterpillar would design and attach its own wings. Just as the caterpillar surrenders to the cocoon and rests in the assurance of what it will become, we need to curl up into God's loving plan for who we are and who we will be.

Connie Neal

*D*eborah is one of several women in Scripture distinguished as being endowed with the prophetic gift, which means the ability to discern the mind and purpose of God and declare it to others. In the days of the Old Testament, prophets and prophetesses were the media between God and his people Israel, and their gift to perceive and proclaim divine truth stamped them as being divinely inspired. Such an office, whether held by a male or female, was a high one and corresponds to the ministry of the Word today. Can you picture how hungry-minded Israelites found their way to that conspicuous palm tree beneath which Deborah sat, stately in person with her dark, penetrating, prophetic eyes, and poured out wisdom and instruction as she declared the whole counsel of God? As a woman, she had intuition as well as inspiration, which is always better than a man's cold reasoning.

Herbert Lockyer

Deborah, a prophetess, the wife of Lappidoth, was leading Israel at that time. She held court under the Palm of Deborah between Ramah and Bethel in the hill country of Ephraim, and the Israelites came to her to have their disputes decided.

Deborah and Barak son of Abinoam sang this song:

"When the princes in Israel take the lead, when the people willingly offer themselves—praise the LORD!

"Hear this, you kings! Listen, you rulers! I will sing to the LORD, I will sing; I will make music to the LORD, the God of Israel.

☜Judges 4:4-5, 5:1–3

God's Grace Extended Through Us

When we receive God's grace in our lives, we can take aim to love one another with the kind of love God gives us—that unconditional agape kind of love. Unconditional love means our Lord doesn't love us only under certain conditions and we need his grace to be filled with that overwhelming power of love we can't provide with our own—far beyond just "being nice" or cordial to others at church. It's more than we can do in our natural strength.

Pat Matuszak

God's love is perfect love embracing the worst in me. It is so hard to comprehend that kind of a love. I'm sure all of us have at times related to the Lord as if he loves like we do—imperfectly; this would include guilt trips, resentment, bitterness, and punishment. I've wasted much time in my relationship with him because I have felt I couldn't approach him. I have kept my distance from the Lord until I felt like I could get back into a right relationship with him or return to his good graces.

But Jesus loves us with an absolute pure love. When I'm finally still, he reveals himself to me, and gives me all I need for righteousness, and a glorious relationship with him. Mercy is waiting to gather you into its arms and remind you of the stubborn love of God.

Kathy Troccoli

Jesus said, "He who receives you receives me, and he who receives me receives the one who sent me. . . . And if anyone gives even a cup of cold water to one of these little ones because he is my disciple, I tell you the truth, he will certainly not lose his reward."

❧Matthew 10:40, 42

Jesus said, "My command is this: Love each other as I have loved you. Greater love has no one than this, that he lay down his life for his friends."

❧John 15:12–13

Above all, love each other deeply, because love covers over a multitude of sins. Offer hospitality to one another without grumbling. Each one should use whatever gift he has received to serve others, faithfully administering God's grace in its various forms. If anyone speaks, he should do it as one speaking the very words of God. If anyone serves, he should do it with the strength God provides, so that in all things God may be praised through Jesus Christ. To him be the glory and the power for ever and ever. Amen.

❧1 Peter 4:8–11

To Our Neighbors and Business Associates

৵

*A*lthough God is real, you can't see him—at least not in this world. Think about what it would be like to have an invisible dance partner. Anyone looking on would see only you and the influence your partner had on you. If he lifted you up and twirled you around, those watching would be astounded because it would look as though you were doing these incredible feats on your own. Yet that is what a relationship with God is like. While you experience his power to move and lift you, others see only you. That's okay. As you continue dancing, others may never see God, but they won't be able to deny what he is doing in your life.

 Connie Neal

Jesus said, "If you love me, you will obey what I command. And I will ask the Father, and he will give you another Counselor to be with you forever — the Spirit of truth. The world cannot accept him, because it neither sees him nor knows him. But you know him, for he lives with you and will be in you. I will not leave you as orphans; I will come to you. Before long, the world will not see me anymore, but you will see me. Because I live, you also will live. On that day you will realize that I am in my Father, and you are in me, and I am in you. Whoever has my commands and obeys them, he is the one who loves me. He who loves me will be loved by my Father, and I too will love him and show myself to him."

❧John 14:15–21

"You are the light of the world. A city on a hill cannot be hidden. Neither do people light a lamp and put it under a bowl. Instead they put it on its stand, and it gives light to everyone in the house. In the same way, let your light shine before men, that they may see your good deeds and praise your Father in heaven."

❧Matthew 5:14–16

I attended a large women's renewal weekend as an observer to write an article for our city newspaper. It really surprised me because it wasn't at all what I expected.

I discovered a group of women doing things they also had not expected—and loving it! They broke out of their comfort zones for a couple of days and found out about women who go to That–Other–Church–Across–Town. For many of them the last thing they expected to do that weekend was have fun—after all isn't spiritual growth an ultra-serious endeavor where you don't ever crack a joke or a smile?

When I sat down in the press area to gather my notes, I met a reporter from a New York women's magazine who was baffled that her editor had asked her to cover this assignment since she herself is Jewish. Obviously in the clutches of a supervisor who wanted her to "grow," she took off for the Midwest with serious misgivings. She said she had expected the event to be more political and contain a long series of rhetorical speeches. At the end of the day, however, she said the conference had been inspiring and that she felt "energized, when I am usually exhausted after this kind of thing."

 Pat Matuszak

With great power the apostles continued to testify to the resurrection of the Lord Jesus, and much grace was upon them all.

❧ Acts 4:33

We believe it is through the grace of our Lord Jesus that we are saved.

❧ Acts 15:11

I consider my life worth nothing to me, if only I may finish the race and complete the task the Lord Jesus has given me — the task of testifying to the gospel of God's grace.

❧ Acts 20:24

Stand firm. Let nothing move you. Always give yourselves fully to the work of the Lord, because you know that your labor in the Lord is not in vain.

❧ 1 Corinthians 15:58

Commit your way to the LORD; trust in him and he will do this: He will make your righteousness shine like the dawn.

❧ Psalm 37:5–6

*J*esus is my beauty. He is my loveliness, my confidence. He is the charisma, the attractiveness that is right and true—that breeds life not death. That points to good and not evil. Jesus. The perfume the world, our family, and our friends will take notice of. What is she wearing? Jesus. The answer must be Jesus.

Mary Magdalene understood the meaning of "wretched woman that I am, but beautiful bride of Christ." She never forgot where she came from, what she was saved from, what she was capable of, and where she'd be without God. But Mary became God's woman, his person, his precious and beautiful bride. Jesus loved her, saved her, believed for her when she didn't even know there was another way, another life, a new and holy journey.

We are all Mary Magdalenes in some sort of way. Wretched women but beautiful brides. Sinners but saved. Broken but beloved. All because he lives in us. Walk confidently this day, knowing that Jesus will shine through you as you look to him.

Kathy Troccoli

This righteousness from God comes through faith in Jesus Christ to all who believe. There is no difference, for all have sinned and fall short of the glory of God, and are justified freely by his grace through the redemption that came by Christ Jesus.

❧Romans 3:22–24

"This, then, is how you should pray: 'Our Father in heaven, hallowed be your name, your kingdom come, your will be done on earth as it is in heaven. Give us today our daily bread. Forgive us our debts, as we also have forgiven our debtors. And lead us not into temptation, but deliver us from the evil one.'"

❧Matthew 6:6, 9–13

*T*rue grace is so overwhelming you are compelled to extend it to those around you, whether they deserve it or not. That is a truly joyful and liberating way to live. Your mind is set; your path is clear; you need not depend on the reactions of others to determine how you will react to them because you have already made your choice. Grace takes the initiative to live with passion and compassion; it does not play it safe, but lavishes itself on others, just as grace is daily lavished on us.

Sheila Walsh

*T*he fear of the LORD is the beginning of wisdom, and knowledge of the Holy One is understanding. For through me your days will be many, and years will be added to your life. If you are wise, your wisdom will reward you.

Proverbs 9:10–12

*Y*ou have a beautiful heart that is loved by the Lord Jesus. That is all you need. For each minute you think you have nothing to give, you lose sixty seconds of giving. So don't wait until your troubles are behind you. The only person whose troubles are behind him is the school bus driver!

Barbara Johnson

Guard your heart, for it is the well-spring of life.

❧Proverbs 4:23

Jesus said, "I am the true vine, and my Father is the gardener. He cuts off every branch in me that bears no fruit, while every branch that does bear fruit he prunes so that it will be even more fruitful."

❧John 15:1–2

Jesus said, "He who receives you receives me, and he who receives me receives the one who sent me."

❧Matthew 10:40

*H*ouse wrens distinguish themselves from other nest builders by a unique habit of over-building. Their custom is that whatever place they select—large, small, or in between—they must fill it completely before it feels "finished." It seems they have no concept of what is enough.

I feel as if I'm looking in the mirror when I read the above description. That's me. If I give away a piece of clothing, I quickly replace it with something new. If I invite guests over for a celebration, I make not one dish but nine.

In Luke 10:38-41, we read the story of Mary and her sister Martha. Jesus has come to visit their home. Both women are excited, but each expresses her welcome in quite a different manner. Mary sits down, focuses her attention on her guest, and listens. She is. Martha mixes a meal for Jesus. She does.

Now, Jesus needed to eat, and someone had to mix the meal. But Martha didn't stop with one course. Instead, she fixed up a feast with preparations that took her solely into the world of doing and out of the sphere of being with her guest. Her actions actually removed her from his presence.

Elisa Morgan

*"M*artha, Martha," the Lord answered, "you are worried and upset about many things, but only one thing is needed."*

Luke 10:41-42

*R*epresent Jesus in your person. Let the world hear him through your voice, see him in your eyes, touch him through your touch, and find him in the treasures of your heart. May we be a book others can't put down until they, too, have put their life and soul into the hands of God.

Kathy Troccoli

A word aptly spoken is like apples of gold in settings of silver.

❧Proverbs 25:11

*W*hen the Holy Spirit gives us the right word at the right time, it is a powerful tool of evangelism. When we immerse ourselves in God's Word, the Spirit can remind us of passages that will have impact in conversation.

❧NIV Christian Growth Study Bible

*B*y the grace of God I am what I am, and his grace to me was not without effect. No, I worked harder than all of them—yet not I, but the grace of God that was with me.

❧1 Corinthians 15:10

You yourselves are our letter, written on our hearts, known and read by everybody. You show that you are a letter from Christ, the result of our ministry, written not with ink but with the Spirit of the living God, not on tablets of stone but on tablets of human hearts. Such confidence as this is ours through Christ before God. Not that we are competent in ourselves to claim anything for ourselves, but our competence comes from God. He has made us competent as ministers of a new covenant—not of the letter but of the Spirit; for the letter kills, but the Spirit gives life.

Now if the ministry that brought death, which was engraved in letters on stone, came with glory, so that the Israelites could not look steadily at the face of Moses because of its glory, fading though it was, will not the ministry of the Spirit be even more glorious?

❧ 2 Corinthians 3:2–8

In the beginning was the Word, and the Word was with God, and the Word was God. He was with God in the beginning. Through him all things were made; without him nothing was made that has been made. In him was life, and that life was the light of men. The light shines in the darkness, but the darkness has not understood it.

❧John 1:1–5

This is how we know what love is: Jesus Christ laid down his life for us. And we ought to lay down our lives for our brothers. If anyone has material possessions and sees his brother in need but has no pity on him, how can the love of God be in him? Dear children, let us not love with words or tongue but with actions and in truth. This then is how we know that we belong to the truth, and how we set our hearts at rest in his presence whenever our hearts condemn us. For God is greater than our hearts, and he knows everything.

❧1 John 3:16–20

Jesus said, "I tell you the truth, anyone who will not receive the kingdom of God like a little child will never enter it."

&Luke 18:17

I took you from the ends of the earth, from its farthest corners I called you. I said, 'You are my servant'; I have chosen you and have not rejected you. So do not fear, for I am with you; do not be dismayed, for I am your God. I will strengthen you and help you; I will uphold you with my righteous right hand.

&Isaiah 41:9–10

"What do you think? If a man owns a hundred sheep, and one of them wanders away, will he not leave the ninety-nine on the hills and go to look for the one that wandered off? And if he finds it, I tell you the truth, he is happier about that one sheep than about the ninety-nine that did not wander off. In the same way your Father in heaven is not willing that any of these little ones should be lost."

&Matthew 18:12–14

To God's Family Around the World

🦋

*L*uke links Mary Magdalene with Joanna and Susanna and "many others": as those "healed of evil spirits and infirmities by Jesus." He saw in her the ministering angel who would be a blessing to his own heart and to others. Mary left her home to follow Jesus. Constantly on the move as Jesus and his disciples were, there were many details in connection with their personal comfort and well-being requiring attention to which these women could see. Quietly and effectively Mary would do what she knew needed to be done. She went with her Lord into the shadows, and is thus represented as being among those who followed Jesus on his last sad journey from Galilee to Jerusalem.

🖼 Herbert Lockyer

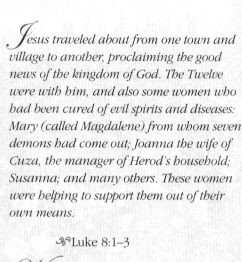

*J*esus traveled about from one town and village to another, proclaiming the good news of the kingdom of God. The Twelve were with him, and also some women who had been cured of evil spirits and diseases: Mary (called Magdalene) from whom seven demons had come out; Joanna the wife of Cuza, the manager of Herod's household; Susanna; and many others. These women were helping to support them out of their own means.

❧Luke 8:1–3

*W*hile a large crowd was gathering and people were coming to Jesus from town after town, he told this parable:
"A farmer went out to sow his seed. As he was scattering the seed, some fell along the path; it was trampled on, and the birds of the air ate it up. Some fell on rock, and when it came up, the plants withered because they had no moisture. Other seed fell among thorns, which grew up with it and choked the plants. Still other seed fell on good soil. It came up and yielded a crop, a hundred times more than was sown." When he said this, he called out, "He who has ears to hear, let him hear."

❧Luke 8:1–8

The first single woman to be commissioned to serve on the foreign field was M. A. Cooke, who responded to a plea from the British and Foreign Bible Society, to establish a school in Calcutta for Hindu girls. Soon after she arrived in India, while she was still in language study, she visited a boys' school to observe their curriculum and teaching methods. There she watched in anguish as the Indian teacher drove away a young girl who was begging to learn to read. The following day, Miss Cooke returned with her interpreter, and immediately gathered together fifteen girls who likewise had been denied education, and there she formed her first mission school.

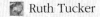 Ruth Tucker

*T*hen Jesus went around teaching from village to village. Calling the Twelve to him, he sent them out two by two and gave them authority over evil spirits. These were his instructions: "Take nothing for the journey except a staff— no bread, no bag, no money in your belts. Wear sandals but not an extra tunic. Whenever you enter a house, stay there until you leave that town. And if any place will not welcome you or listen to you, shake the dust off your feet when you leave, as a testimony against them." They went out and preached that people should repent. They drove out many demons and anointed many sick people with oil and healed them.

ȘMark 6:6-13

*W*e are therefore Christ's ambassadors, as though God were making his appeal through us. We implore you on Christ's behalf: Be reconciled to God. God made him who had no sin to be sin for us, so that in him we might become the right-eousness of God. As God's fellow workers we urge you not to receive God's grace in vain. For he says, "In the time of my favor I heard you, and in the day of salvation I helped you." I tell you, now is the time of God's favor, now is the day of salvation.

Ș2 Corinthians 5:20–6:2

"*You* are the light of the world," Jesus said. (Matthew 5:14). What a startling statement to make! Surely only Jesus is what he stated about himself, "I am the light of the world. Whoever follows me will never walk in darkness, but will have the light of life" (John 8:12).

Amazingly, Jesus also announced to his disciples, "You are the salt of the earth" (Matthew 5:13). The salt referred to here is not the purified salt obtained through evaporation, but rather a rock salt used to lightly spread on soil to fertilize it for greater fruitfulness.

Further, God says that his people are "a letter from Christ . . . written not with ink, but with the Spirit of the living God . . . on tablets of human hearts" (2 Corinthians 3:3).

What substance constitutes light, salt and words that can literally carve themselves into the very flesh of the human heart? Jesus gives us the answer in John 6:63: "The words that I have spoken to you are spirit and they are life." How then, can we be the lights of the world, the savory salt, the letter of Christ? Only as his Word lives inside us and is passed on to others.

International Bible Society
Call to Prayer, May 25, 1999

Jesus said, "You are the salt of the earth. But if the salt loses its saltiness, how can it be made salty again? It is no longer good for anything, except to be thrown out and trampled by men. You are the light of the world. A city on a hill cannot be hidden. Neither do people light a lamp and put it under a bowl. Instead they put it on its stand, and it gives light to everyone in the house.
In the same way, let your light shine before men, that they may see your good deeds and praise your Father in heaven."

ॐMatthew 5:13–16

You yourselves are our letter, written on our hearts, known and read by everybody. You show that you are a letter from Christ, the result of our ministry, written not with ink but with the Spirit of the living God, not on tablets of stone but on tablets of human hearts. Such confidence as this is ours through Christ before God.

ॐ2 Corinthians 3:2

*I*s not this the kind of fasting I have chosen: to loose the chains of injustice and untie the cords of the yoke, to set the oppressed free and break every yoke? Is it not to share your food with the hungry and to provide the poor wanderer with shelter—when you see the naked, to clothe him, and not to turn away from your own flesh and blood? Then your light will break forth like the dawn, and your healing will quickly appear; then your righteousness will go before you, and the glory of the LORD will be your rear guard.

The LORD will guide you always; he will satisfy your needs in a sun-scorched land and will strengthen your frame. You will be like a well-watered garden, like a spring whose waters never fail.

❧Isaiah 58:6–8,11

*S*piritual renewal includes carrying out compassionate acts for other. If we focus our attention on our own lives and ignore others, we will not progress in our spiritual growth. God urges us to love others and treat them justly.

❧NIV Spiritual Renewal Bible

*A*my Carmichael was probably the most famous single woman missionary to leave the shores of England in the modern missionary period. Her thirty-five books detailing her more than fifty years in India were widely read in Christian circles in England as well as America. In India, Carmichael became deeply involved in children's work, most specifically in rescuing girls from temple prostitution. She established a home and school for these children. It became known as Dohnavur Fellowship. This all-consuming ministry became her life, and the staff and children were her family. By 1952 the "family" numbered nine hundred.

Ruth A. Tucker

The quiet words of the wise are more to be heeded than the shouts of a ruler of fools. Wisdom is better than weapons of war.

Ecclesiastes 9:17–18

Jesus said, "When the Son of Man comes in his glory, and all the angels with him, he will sit on his throne in heavenly glory. All the nations will be gathered before him, and he will separate the people one from another as a shepherd separates the sheep from the goats. He will put the sheep on his right and the goats on his left.

Then the King will say to those on his right, 'Come, you who are blessed by my Father; take your inheritance, the kingdom prepared for you since the creation of the world. For I was hungry and you gave me something to eat, I was thirsty and you gave me something to drink, I was a stranger and you invited me in, I needed clothes and you clothed me, I was sick and you looked after me, I was in prison and you came to visit me.'

"Then the righteous will answer him, 'Lord, when did we see you hungry and feed you, or thirsty and give you something to drink? When did we see you a stranger and invite you in, or needing clothes and clothe you? When did we see you sick or in prison and go to visit you?'

"The King will reply, 'I tell you the truth, whatever you did for one of the least of these brothers of mine, you did for me.'"

❧Matthew 25:31–40

If the sun doesn't shine I have a flashlight—God's word is a lamp unto my feet guiding my every step; his eyes seeing for me when I am too blind to see; his fire setting my heart ablaze so that I can see my sin and allow his love to consume it. The sweet glow of his presence shines into my darkness. His touch is upon my pain. His mercy covers me. And as I have received, I can give; I can hold out my flashlight, enabling others to see and be comforted when the sun is not shining and the days are like nights.

We must not sit in the dark. We must remember what we have in him. His light and his love are ever shining.

Kathy Troccoli

God, who said, "Let light shine out of darkness," made his light shine in our hearts to give us the light of the knowledge of the glory of God in the face of Christ. But we have this treasure in jars of clay to show that this all-surpassing power is from God and not from us.

2 Corinthians 4:6–7

Then the disciples went out and preached everywhere, and the Lord worked with them and confirmed his word by the signs that accompanied it.

❧Mark 16:20

We will discover that the power of Jesus' resurrection will touch and transform our lives. Then we can become a source of encouragement to others as we share the story of God's transforming power.

❧NIV Spiritual Formation Bible

God raised us up with Christ and seated us with him in the heavenly realms in Christ Jesus, in order that in the coming ages he might show the incomparable riches of his grace, expressed in his kindness to us in Christ Jesus.

❧Ephesians 2:6

Now the Lord is the Spirit, and where the Spirit of the Lord is, there is freedom. And we, who with unveiled faces all reflect the Lord's glory, are being transformed into his likeness with ever-increasing glory, which comes from the Lord, who is the Spirit. Therefore, since through God's mercy we have this ministry, we do not lose heart.

❧2 Corinthians 3:17–18

There's a wideness in God's mercy,
Like the wideness of the sea;
There's a kindness in his justice,
Which is more than liberty

There is welcome for the sinner,
And more graces for the good;
There is mercy with the Savior;
There is healing in his blood.

For the love of God is broader
Than the measure of one's mind;
And the heart of the Eternal
Is most wonderfully kind.

If our love were but more simple,
We could take him at his word;
And our lives would be more loving
In the likeness of our Lord.

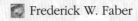 Frederick W. Faber

*E*ach one should use whatever gift he has received to serve others, faithfully administering God's grace in it's various forms. If anyone speaks, he should do it as one speaking the very words of God. If anyone serves, he should do it with the strength God provides so that in all things God may be praised through Jesus Christ. To him be the glory and the power forever and ever. Amen.

❧ 1 Peter 4:10–11

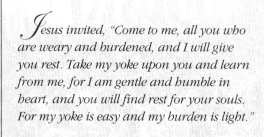

Jesus invited, "Come to me, all you who are weary and burdened, and I will give you rest. Take my yoke upon you and learn from me, for I am gentle and humble in heart, and you will find rest for your souls. For my yoke is easy and my burden is light."

❧Matthew 11:28

Sources

Baldwin, Carol L. *Women's Devotional Bible*. (Grand Rapids: ZondervanPublishingHouse, 1990).

Barnes, M. Craig. Hustling God: *Why We Work So Hard for What God Wants to Give*. (Grand Rapids: ZondervanPublishing House, 1999).

Peggy Benson, Sue Buchanan, Gloria Gaither, Joy MacKenzie. *Friends Through Thick and Thin*. (Grand Rapids: Zondervan PublishingHouse, 1998).

Bush, Barbara. *Heart Trouble*. (Grand Rapids: Zondervan PublishingHouse, 1981).

Chapian, Marie. *Women's Devotional Bible*. (Grand Rapids: ZondervanPublishingHouse, 1990).

Patsy Clairmont, Barbara Johnson, Marilyn Meberg, Luci Swindoll, Sheila Walsh, Thelma Wells. *Outrageous Joy. OverJoyed!* (Grand Rapids: ZondervanPublishingHouse, 1999).

Cowman, L.B. *Streams in the Desert*. (Grand Rapids: Zondervan PublishingHouse, 1998).

Dravecky, Jan. *A Joy I'd Never Known*. (Grand Rapids: ZondervanPublishingHouse, 1996).

Herbert Lockyer. *All the Women of the Bible*. (Grand Rapids: ZondervanPublishingHouse, 1990).

MacDonald, Hope. *When Angels Appear*. (Grand Rapids: ZondervanPublishingHouse, 1982).

Morgan, Elisa. *Meditations for Mothers*. (Grand Rapids: ZondervanPublishingHouse, 1999).

Debbie Morris. *Forgiving the Dead Man Walking*. (Grand Rapids: ZondervanPublishingHouse, 1999).

Neal, Connie. *Dancing In the Arms of God*. (Grand Rapids: ZondervanPublishingHouse, 1995).

Spangler, Ann. *An Angel a Day: Stories of Angelic Encounters*. (Grand Rapids: ZondervanPublishingHouse, 1994).

Tada, Joni Eareckson. *When God Weeps*. (Grand Rapids: ZondervanPublishingHouse, 1998). *A Step Further*. (Grand Rapids: ZondervanPublishingHouse, 1978).

Tirabassi, Becky. *Wild Things Happen When I Pray*. (Grand Rapids: ZondervanPublishingHouse, 1994).

Kathy Troccoli. *My Life Is in Your Hands*. (Grand Rapids: ZondervanPublishingHouse, 1997).

Ruth A. Tucker and Walter L. Liefeld. *Daughters of the Church*. (Grand Rapids: ZondervanPublishingHouse, 1987).

Walsh, Sheila. *Honestly*. (Grand Rapids: ZondervanPublishing House, 1998).